# JEAN ANOUILH

## *Stages in Rebellion*

I am the unhappiest of men, but also one who takes his misfortunes better than anyone else: I was born with the gift of transforming them into laughter.

(Anouilh, *Cher Antoine*)

I rebel, therefore we are.

(Camus, *L'Homme révolté*)

# JEAN ANOUILH

## *Stages in Rebellion*

By

### B. A. LENSKI

HUMANITIES PRESS       Atlantic Highlands, N.J.

1975

Library of Congress Cataloging in Publication Data

Lenski, B. A.
Jean Anouilh; stages in rebellion.

Bibliography: p.
1. Anouilh, Jean, 1910–
PQ2601.N67Z67      842'.9'14      73-12687
ISBN 0-391-00323-2

Printed in the United States of America

# CONTENTS

Page

1. GRADUS AD PARNASSUM . . . . . . . . . . . . . . . . . . . . .1

2. REBELLION AGAINST TIME . . . . . . . . . . . . . . . . . .17

3. REBELLION AGAINST ENVIRONMENT . . . . . . . . . .25

4. REBELLION FOR A CAUSE . . . . . . . . . . . . . . . . . . .35

5. HISTORICAL REBELLION . . . . . . . . . . . . . . . . . . . .47

6. REBELLION WITHOUT A CAUSE . . . . . . . . . . . . . . .58

7. REBELLION OF THE ARTIST . . . . . . . . . . . . . . . . . .67

8. CONCLUSION . . . . . . . . . . . . . . . . . . . . . . . . . . . . .73

9. AN ALPHABET OF ANOUILH . . . . . . . . . . . . . . . . .81

Notes and References . . . . . . . . . . . . . . . . . . . . . . . . . . . .91

Chronology of Theatrical Productions . . . . . . . . . . . . . . .99

Published Plays . . . . . . . . . . . . . . . . . . . . . . . . . . . . . . .102

Selected Bibliography . . . . . . . . . . . . . . . . . . . . . . . . . . .104

## 1. GRADUS AD PARNASSUM

*From the Arcachon Casino
to the Atelier (1910-1940)*

Jean Anouilh was born on June 23, 1910, in Bordeaux. His father, François Anouilh, was a tailor; his mother, Marie-Magdeleine née Soulue, was a violinist in the Arcachon Casino, which was managed by a relative. At eight, the young boy discovered the world of musical comedy at the casino. At ten, he was writing plays in verse. His idol was Rostand, and the hero looming behind most of the protagonists in his own juvenile dramatic ventures was inevitably Cyrano de Bergerac. The indomitable spirit of Cyrano has never entirely disappeared from Anouilh's theatrical universe.

In his early teens, Anouilh moved to Paris where he completed the elementary grades and attended the Collège Chaptal. At fifteen, he began to haunt the Parisian theatres and, at sixteen, he wrote his first full-length play in prose in emulation of Henry Bataille, *La Femme sur la cheminée*. The play is about a man who overly respects a woman and who becomes the victim of his idolatry. It is interesting to note that the theme of love's fallacy, so dear to Anouilh, appears this early in his playwriting.

1

During his Collège Chaptal years, there was scarcely a top balcony in which Anouilh did not stand, engrossed in the fabulous dream-and-yet-real world of the stage. It was as if he were waiting for a message, or perhaps a revelation. For Anouilh, the Paris of 1925 was a place of perpetual enchantment, a city where great actors and directors passed by in the street, where theatres sparkled with promise in the evenings. On the Dancourt Square, in the heart of Montmartre, the fifteen-year-old Anouilh waited with a friend after a performance to see the great Dullin exit from the Atelier theatre, step into his unusual horse-driven carriage and disappear into the night. In that year, Jouvet presented Crommelynck and Vildrac at the Comédie des Champs-Elysées; Pitoëff introduced Pirandello's *Henry IV* to the Parisian public; and Gaston Baty offered Strindberg's *Miss Julie*. Two years later, Pitoëff, Jouvet, Dullin and Baty joined forces in founding the famous "Cartel des Quatre." This was 1927, and Anouilh, a voracious reader of Molière, Musset, Marivaux, Shaw, Claudel and Pirandello, was in his last year at the Collège Chaptal.

Jean-Louis Barrault, who was also born in 1910 and who also attended the Collège Chaptal, recalls the Anouilh of 1927 as a somewhat distant boy. At that time, there was no rapport between Barrault and Anouilh. Barrault was a nervous, temperamental youth, who made his companions laugh with his funny grimaces and his gift for mimicry. Anouilh was just the opposite, a grown-up man at seventeen, a stern observer of the world around him.

In 1927, Anouilh graduated from Chaptal in the humanities division, after which he enrolled at the University of Paris to study law. The next year an event took place that was to determine the course of his career: Anouilh saw Giraudoux's *Siegfried,* first performed on May 3, 1928, at the Comédie des Champs-Elysées under the direction of Louis Jouvet. Giraudoux revealed to Anouilh that poetic and artificial language rings truer on stage than conversation faithfully transcribed. *Humulus le muet,* a very short play written in 1929 in collaboration with Jean Aurenche, is Anouilh's first attempt at putting into practice the important lesson learned from Giraudoux.

At the time of *Humulus,* Anouilh was still a law student. One scarcely imagines the future author of *Le Bal des voleurs, Colombe* and *La Valse des toréadors* seated in the classrooms of the Faculty of Law preparing for a legal career. That year, after having maintained matriculation for over eighteen months, Anouilh abruptly quit his studies, obliged by precarious financial conditions to find a white-collar job. He joined the influential Damour advertising company in a clerical capacity and spent the next two years writing publicity to help sell a variety of goods from automobiles to underwear. He worked on the first publicity films made in Europe. To supplement his salary, he wrote comic gags for films. Looking back on these days, Anouilh has come to regard them as having provided excellent experience in concise writing. Producing advertising slogans taught him the precision which characterizes the sentences he was to write for the stage.

In 1931, after two years of underpaid hard work, Anouilh left Damour and became secretary of Louis Jouvet's company. Jouvet thought very little of Anouilh as a would-be author. He followed his secretary's dramatic efforts with amusement. The great French actor and director liked to tease Anouilh for being so ambitious in a field for which he considered him only less than moderately gifted. Jouvet looked upon Anouilh as an ordinary member of his staff who happened to have had useful experience in advertising. In his own way, however, Jouvet was quite generous. When Anouilh married Monelle Valentin, a young and penniless actress he met during his advertising days, Jouvet lent the young couple, hardly in a position to buy real furniture, the stage sets of that same *Siegfried* over which Anouilh had shed tears in 1928, stipulating that this ersatz-furniture be returned to the Comédie des Champs-Elysées at the latest on the occasion of the play's revival.

In 1932, Pierre Fresnay succeeded in persuading Lugné-Poe, the then famous director of the Théâtre de l'Oeuvre who had been the first to introduce Jarry, Claudel, Crommelynck and Salacrou to the French public, to add the name of Anouilh to his impressive list of first offerings.

*L'Hermine,* written in 1931, was performed at the Théâtre de l'Oeuvre on April 26, 1932, with Pierre Fresnay in the role of Frantz. The play closed after thirty-seven performances. The critics took note of the talent of the young playwright. Not much more was said, but even this modest success sufficed to determine Anouilh to leave Jouvet, whom he did not like, in order to devote himself to his one real vocation.

Between 1932 and 1935, the year of his first financial success, Anouilh lived in poverty. Among the scanty biographical bits available concerning these three years, one stands out: when a daughter was born to Jean and Monelle in 1934, little Catherine Anouilh spent the first months of her life in a suitcase.

Anouilh worked hard to earn a better living for his family, and each play he completed gave him new hope. In 1932, Anouilh wrote *Jézabel* and *Le Bal des voleurs.* In 1933, *Mandarine,* a 1929 play dating from the Damour days, was

performed at L'Athénée. It closed after thirteen performances. Anouilh went on writing persistently. In 1934, he
finished *La Sauvage* and *Y avait un prisonnier.*

Anouilh had particularly high hopes for *Le Bal des voleurs,* a "comédie-ballet" filled with gaiety and youthful
exuberance, geared to appeal to the boulevard public. But
one director after another turned it down, along with other
plays submitted by the little-known author whose record of
previously performed plays inspired but little confidence.
Then came the first important break. Le Théâtre des Ambassadeurs accepted *Y avait un prisonnier.* The first performance
took place on March 18, 1935, and the play ran for over two
months. In spite of some excellent reviews, the play failed to
draw the public, and Anouilh's chances of improving his
standard of living looked as slim as ever, when something
short of a miracle took place. Metro-Goldwyn-Mayer purchased the movie rights for *Y avait un prisonnier* and its fee,
translated into French money and seen from the perspective
of a poor playwright, amounted to a small fortune. At that
moment of his life, Anouilh could not have wished for more
than suddenly came to him from the least expected source:
the gift of time and independence from financial worries and
an impetus for new work. Little Catherine was taken out of
her suitcase and placed in a real bed; a new home could be
afforded; and, most spectacular of all, Anouilh bought a
convertible automobile. Thus he and Monelle drove off hap-
pily one morning, under the suspicious gaze of the concierge,
headed for an exciting exploration of roadside France.

It was American money that opened up bright perspectives for Anouilh's creative work. Three of his plays had been
produced in Paris with hardly any financial reward, when,
ironically, the key to fortune, and perhaps to glory, was given

Anouilh for the rights to a movie that has never been made. All that Anouilh needed now was more substantial recognition by the critics and the public, a goal achieved in 1937. In the early part of that year Anouilh met Georges Pitoëff, the indefatigable actor, director and producer, and his wife Ludmilla, the great actress who accompanied her husband on his numerous tours, ranging as far as Siberia. A friendship and collaboration developed from their meeting which set Anouilh on the way to fame. In the Paris Théâtre des Mathurins, on April 10, 1937, Georges Pitoëff presented *Le Voyageur sans bagage,* completed by Anouilh the previous year. The play had considerable success, both with the critics and the public and ran for almost two hundred performances. Shortly after *Le Voyageur sans bagage* closed, Pitoëff staged another play by Anouilh, *La Sauvage,* which had been turned down by a number of directors since its writing in 1934. The first performance took place on January 10, 1938. Georges Pitoëff, who directed the play, appeared on stage in the role of Florent, opposite Ludmilla's Thérèse. The heated discussions with Georges during rehearsals, Milhaud's music for the stage, Ludmilla's magnificent intonations while playing "la sauvage," as well as so many other things evoking the Mathurins evenings, remain unforgettable for Anouilh. He grew to feel deep admiration for Georges and Ludmilla. In his eyes, they were the incarnation of the united couple, so exalted by Giraudoux and vainly sought after by many of the young lovers in Anouilh's own plays. They were almost the embodiment of a human Androgyne.

In the summer of 1937, another important meeting that was to help shape Anouilh's fame took place. That summer, he and Monelle were winding their way through Brittany by car in search of a house to rent. Anouilh hated to write in

Paris, particularly during the summer. As long as he had been bound to the city by poverty he had not been able to help doing so, but from the moment *Y avait un prisonnier* set him free, he insisted on doing all his writing in the country.

Although financially stable, the Anouilhs were still far from well off and hardly could afford to be extravagant. Their aspirations for the month of August were limited to a small house not too squalid and not too far from the sea. The Breton real estate agents to whom they described this ideal summer place mortified them with their disdain. As they went from one to another, describing their needs with increasing humility, they met men from whom the vestiges of humaneness seemed drained. Disgusted with the Breton realtors, Anouilh decided to return to Paris, in 1937 the site of the World's Fair. But as soon as he entered the city he wondered why he had returned. The Fair did not interest him in the least, and Paris in August was certainly not the ideal place to be. Then one night he went to the Comédie des Champs-Elysées, where nine years earlier he had seen *Siegfried,* and he knew right away why he had come back. He had come to see Carlo Gozzi's fairy play, *Le Roi Cerf,* performed by André Barsacq and his small "Troupe des Quatre-Saisons." After the performance he went backstage to congratulate Barsacq on his achievement. From the style displayed by the ensemble, he could visualize the troupe performing *Le Bal des voleurs.* After overcoming the shyness they had in common, the two men discovered that they shared a good many other things, above all a boundless zest for the theatre and high hopes for the future. On their first meeting, amid the sets of *Le Roi Cerf,* it was as if a pact had been sealed. Anouilh gave Barsacq *Le Bal des voleurs* to read, and Barsacq was enchanted, after which all that there remained for them

to do was to leave on vacation together and spend the rest of
the summer in Erqui, a small coastal town in the north of
Brittany. There, to the surprise of sunbathers, Anouilh and
Barsacq, drunk with joy, held the first limited rehearsal of *Le
Bal des voleurs,* improvising the pantomime of the thieves,
dancing and jumping in the sand. The first real performance
of the play by "La Troupe des Quatre-Saisons" under the
direction of Barsacq took place a year later, on September
17, 1938, at the Théâtre des Arts. Before *Le Bal des voleurs*
opened, Anouilh had already written a new play which he
was eager to see performed, *Le Rendez-vous de Senlis.* He
had met Jean-Louis Barrault and mentioned the play to him.
Barrault had shown an interest in the play and invited
Anouilh to his home for a reading.

Eleven years had passed since the Chaptal days when
Barrault and Anouilh had known each other by sight. Although in those days they had seemed to have nothing in
common, in 1938 they might well have established their first
artistic relationship. Anouilh went to Barrault's home with
*Le Rendez-vous de Senlis.* He began reading. However, it
happened that Barrault had a friend in his apartment who
was seriously ill, and, consequently, he found it hard to
concentrate on the reading and listened to Anouilh dis-
tractedly. He liked the first act, but by the time Anouilh had
finished reading it, Barrault was so nervous that he explained
to the impassioned playwright, who was prepared to read all
night if necessary, that, due to the exceptional circumstances,
he would rather keep the manuscript and read it himself.
Anouilh left the manuscript, but the next day Barrault received a telegram asking him in clear-cut terms to return *Le
Rendez-vous de Senlis* immediately. It was an unfortunate
encounter. Anouilh was offended, and instead of going to
Barrault, the play went to Barsacq.

*Le Bal des voleurs* ran for 200 performances at the Théâtre des Arts, closing early in spring 1939, the year in which Anouilh wrote *Léocadia,* which was performed during the war, in November 1940, at the Théâtre de la Michodière with Pierre Fresnay in the role of the Prince and Yvonne Printemps in the role of Amanda, with stage music by Francis Poulenc.

## The Road to Fame (1940–    )

During the four-year period of the Occupation, Anouilh and Barsacq's alliance was conclusively established when Barsacq became director of the Atelier theatre, entrusted to him by Dullin at the end of 1940.[1] For a new and auspicious beginning at the Atelier, Barsacq revived *Le Bal des voleurs,* followed by *Le Rendez-vous de Senlis* in 1941, *Eurydice* in 1942 and *Antigone* in 1944. The most memorable date of this period at the Atelier was February 4, 1944, the evening of the first performance of *Antigone,* the play that propelled Anouilh to international fame. Barsacq recalls the evening as a unique theatrical experience. Never before had he seen an audience so spellbound by a play, the effectiveness of which was enhanced by the choice of modern costumes, designed to create a symphony of black and white.

*Antigone's* magnetic appeal for the public was due in part to the times in which the play was performed. Certain passages of *Antigone* were inevitably interpreted in the light of historical and political events. To some of those who sympathized with or actively participated in the Resistance, Anouilh seemed too lenient with Creon "the collaborationist." Anouilh was not well regarded by the underground press, and Sartre in particular, committed as he was to political participation, had little esteem for Anouilh's Olympian attitude toward politics, and for what a critic calls

Anouilh's "anarchic pessimism."[2] On the other hand, to the collaborationist faithful to the Vichy Government of Pétain, Antigone appeared too great a trouble-maker and revolutionary, and Anouilh found himself attacked from that quarter as well.

In the midst of turbulent events and changing political perspectives—during the Normandy landing, the battle of France and the several months following the Liberation of Paris—*Antigone* enjoyed a continuous triumphant run of close to 500 performances.

After the Liberation, Anouilh and Barsacq's association continued for several more years with the following plays staged at the Atelier: *Roméo et Jeannette* in 1946, *L'Invitation au château* in 1947, *Colombe* in 1951 and *Médée* in 1953, the year when Anouilh, upon divorcing Monelle Valentin, married Marie Lançon, another actress.

After *Médée,* Anouilh took his plays to the Comédie des Champs-Elysées and the Théâtre Montparnasse-Gaston Baty.[3] During the fifties, Anouilh wrote more plays than could be absorbed by one theatre alone. Since nearly each of his plays was assured a long run, there were times when two or even three of his plays were being performed simultaneously. Anouilh's switch from the Atelier to the Comédie des Champs-Elysées also coincides with the growing fame of the author, who by the time of *L'Alouette* was considered by many as the greatest contemporary French dramatist.

The collaboration between Anouilh and Barsacq had lasted for almost fifteen years. By the time it ended, it had already gone down in the history of the modern French theatre as a great author-director alliance of equal stature with the Giraudoux-Jouvet and Claudel-Barrault teams.

In 1950, Anouilh wrote *La Répétition ou L'Amour puni,*

a play revolving around the rehearsal of another play, Marivaux's *La Double Inconstance*. With the outstanding 1946 production of Marivaux's *Les Fausses Confidences* at the Marigny theatre, Barrault had acquired the reputation of Marivaux specialist. No wonder Anouilh, always anxious to secure the best possible staging for each of his plays, sent *La Répétition* to him. During rehearsals, Anouilh often proved exasperating for the Madeleine-Renaud—Jean-Louis Barrault troupe. Remembering the questionable impression Barrault had left on him in 1938, and for years accustomed to an almost perfect association with Barsacq, Anouilh lacked complete confidence in Barrault. Only after the triumphant success of *La Répétition* did he cast aside his last doubts about Barrault's competence as a director.

The collaboration between Anouilh and Barrault was renewed in 1959 when, at the Festival in Anouilh's native Bordeaux and later at the Théâtre de France, Barrault presented *La Petite Molière*, a play, originally conceived as a movie scenario in collaboration with Roland Laudenbach, depicting the life and struggles of Molière.

In 1959, twenty-three years after his breakthrough with *Le Voyageur sans bagage*, Anouilh occupied an enviable position. That year, three of his plays were performed simultaneously in three different Parisian theatres: *L'Hurluberlu ou Le Réactionnaire amoureux* at the Comédie des Champs-Elysées, *La Petite Molière* in the Théâtre de France and *Becket ou L'Honneur de Dieu* in the Théâtre Montparnasse-Gaston Baty. Anouilh himself directed *Becket* and received for it the Prix Dominique for the year's most eminent stage direction.

In 1960, La Table Ronde published the sixth volume of Anouilh's collected plays, *Pièces costumées*, after previously having brought out volumes entitled *Pièces roses, Pièces noires, Nouvelles Pièces noires, Pièces brillantes* and *Pièces grinçantes.*

In addition to writing plays, Anouilh has done several screen and stage adaptations and since *Becket* in 1959, has been active not only directing his own plays (*Le Songe du critique, La Grotte, L'Orchestre, La Foire d'Empoigne*) but also was hailed by the critics in 1960 for his outstanding stage direction of the Comédie des Champs-Elysées presentation of Molière's *Tartuffe* and in 1962 of the Théâtre de L'Ambigu revival of Roger Vitrac's *Victor ou Les Enfants au pouvoir.* In 1962, La Table Ronde brought out Anouilh's *Fables,* a collection of fables much in the vein of La Fontaine, filled with satirical comments on contemporary life.

After *La Foire d'Empoigne* (1962), for nearly six years no new play by Anouilh was performed in Paris. Anouilh's adaptation of Shakespeare's *Richard III* was produced in 1964; his adaptation of Kleist's *La Petite Cathrine de Heilbronn,* in 1966. Starting with the 1968 performance of *Le Boulanger, la Boulangère et le Petit Mitron,* Anouilh again began turning out new plays at the rate to which he had accustomed the Parisian public in the past. In 1970, La Table Ronde published *Les Nouvelles Pièces grinçantes,* the seventh volume of his collected plays.

When asked about his life, Anouilh likes to invoke his right to absolute privacy. In an often-quoted letter to a critic, having yielded for once to a request for biographical data, after having disclosed the date of his birth, the names of the schools he had attended and little more, Anouilh concluded: "The rest is my life, and for as long as heaven grant me that it remain my private affair, I shall keep the details to myself."[4] He exasperates interviewers and newspapermen with his stubborn refusal to discuss practically anything about himself that they do not already know. André Parinaud, who, like so many others, was unable to extract much from Anouilh, speaks of Anouilh's sensitivity, reticence, mistrustfulness and refusal to meet people he does not like, so as to spare them the look in the eyes which always gives him away.[5] "Anouilh is not talkative, once it comes down to himself, his life, and even his work," writes Roland Laudenbach.[6]

These observations coincide with Barrault's recollections of Anouilh at the Collège Chaptal as a distant little man and the impressions of Marcel Aymé, who draws attention to Anouilh's remote attitude not only toward the people with whom he comes into contact but toward the period of history in which he lives. Aymé alludes to Anouilh's preference for the *Ancien Régime,* the Proustian and Victorian eras and concludes that Anouilh's severity toward the world of today is manifest both in his plays and in his personal attitude.[7] Alluding to the close relationship between the man and his work, with *L'Hurluberlu* particularly in mind, Aymé suggests that a good approach to Anouilh's biography lies, not in useless interviews but in the plays themselves. Luppé finds in Anouilh's secretiveness the need to save himself for his plays.[8]

A biography of Anouilh based on his works has yet to be compiled. The orchestra platforms in *La Sauvage* and *L'Orchestre* where musicians, eager to stay in the good graces of Monsieur Lebonze, perform under the permanent threat of broken contracts, point to Anouilh's childhood memories centered around the Arcachon Casino where Mme Marie-Magdeleine Anouilh played the violin to help support the family. The passage from *La Sauvage* in which Florent expresses admiration for the miraculous survival of Thérèse's soul despite her long affiliation with the orchestra, acquires

particular meaning when applied to Anouilh's own early
struggles. "It could have made her niggardly, but instead it
adorned her with strength, sincerity, with a kind of virility"
(154).*

One can only speculate about the parallel between André
Bitos' evocation of his school days in *Pauvre Bitos ou le
Dîner de têtes* and Anouilh's own memories of the Collège
Chaptal. Did Anouilh, the son of a tailor and an Arcachon
Casino violinist, suffer from the contempt of a group of rich
boys, as did Bitos, the washer-woman's son? Did he, like
Bitos, harden and adopt a stern, distant mask as a weapon
against the hostility he met? Did he, like Bitos, seek compen-
sation in hard work and professional affirmation for a lack of
popularity and revenge for the lost opportunities that are the
birthright of the rich? And later in life, after having become
rich and widely acclaimed, did he feel sufficiently rewarded
and able to forego all regrets, or did he find himself like
Mignard in *La Petite Molière* "alone like a rat, at the side of
his purse, with his awkwardness at living."[9]

* * * * * * *

A study of Anouilh's theatre discloses Anouilh's changing
perspectives.

Present in all his theatre is Anouilh's awareness of the
absurd, a feeling resulting from the difficulties encountered
by a person seeking clarity and harmony in an irrational
universe in which nature and other people conspire against

---

*The page numbers in parentheses following quotations correspond to
page numbers in the editions of Anouilh's works listed at the end of
the book. The translations are mine.

individual strivings and in which time ultimately crushes everything. Those who experience the absurd must learn how to live with it. The answers to the absurd range from suicide to metaphysical and historical rebellion.

Anouilh's awareness of the absurd is already manifest in *Humulus le muet,* a fifteen-minute burlesque occasionally performed by amateur groups. Humulus is a young man with a unique kind of muteness. He possesses the capacity of saying one word per day, and when he remains silent for twenty-four hours, the following day he can utter two. Ordinarily, his daily utterances are used in pleasing his grandmother, the duchess, with an appropriate word carefully chosen by his tutor for each occasion. Once yearly, Humulus is expected to remain silent for three days so that on his grandmother's birthday he can utter the family slogan "Honor Above All." One year, however, Humulus suddenly retreats into prolonged silence. He not only refuses to utter his customary daily word, but when the time comes, even the family slogan. He has fallen in love with a girl and decided to remain silent for thirty days in a row in order to accumulate enough words to make a love declaration. On the thirtieth day, ecstatic after his long anticipation, Humulus finally emits his thirty words, only to learn that the girl has not understood him because she is almost deaf. When she lifts her earphone and asks him to repeat himsef, he has no words left and is reduced to final despair. He will need another thirty days to save up a new supply of words, and when he meets the girl again, he most likely will fail again in his attempt to be understood.

Humulus' wasted effort brings to mind the image of Sisyphus repeatedly pushing his stone toward the top of a mountain. Patiently, Humulus "pushes" his words toward the peak of a declaration, only to see, when he is on the verge of attaining his goal, the result of much effort vanish into an abyss of non-comprehension.

When confronted with Anouilh's theatrical universe, one is invited from the outset to witness the striving of the heroes to go beyond the absurd in their search of valid reasons for living. In the *Pièces roses* and *Pièces brillantes,* Anouilh's heroes seek "eternity" in a fleeting moment of love and inevitably fail in their futile rebellion against time. In the *Pièces noires,* they resent their environments and seek a reason for which to live in a partner who would totally understand them and who would relieve them of their suffering by sharing it. Since, as the *Pièces noires* reveal, such ideal partners do not exist, the hopes of the heroes who search for them are bound to end in disillusionment. Starting with *Antigone* and later *L'Alouette* and *Becket* Anouilh's heroes are rebels for a cause, adopting a different attitude with which to counteract the absurd: they build their own mountains.

In an examination of Anouilh's theatre through various stages of rebellion, we will find Anouilh's heroes, like the author himself, loving, searching, playing, aging, giving their all and observing a world in which there is a permanent struggle between light and darkness, the *rose* and the *noir,* the *brillant* and the *grinçant,* the heart and reason, the *nu* and the *costumé.*

O time, suspend your flight!
And you, propitious hours,
Suspend your course . . .
(Lamartine)

## 2. REBELLION AGAINST TIME: *PIÈCES ROSES, PIÈCES BRILLANTES* AND TWO *PIÈCES GRINÇANTES*

In the *Pièces roses, Pièces brillantes* and two of the *Pièces grinçantes* (*Ardèle* and *La Valse des toréadors*),[1] the settings, with very few exceptions, have one thing in common: they represent places far removed from the turmoil of reality. A castle is the setting for *Léocadia, L'Invitation au château* and *La Répétition;* a theatre, for *Colombe;* a general's provincial home, for *Ardèle* and *La Valse des toréadors.* In *Le Bal des voleurs,* we see an old-fashioned drawing room in the villa of an extravagant old lady; in *Le Rendez-vous de Senlis,* a rococo drawing room in a house several miles outside Paris, rented to serve as a secluded spot for a lovers' meeting.[2]

Anouilh puts his lovers in these closed-in worlds where—from *Le Bal des voleurs* to *La Valse des toréadors*—we witness their quest for happiness through love, conducted, as a rule, by the male protagonists whose female counterparts in the *Pièces roses* and *Pièces brillantes* are, without exception, young working-class girls invited into a milieu very different from their own. Isabelle in *Le Rendez-vous de Senlis,* Amanda in *Léocadia,* Isabelle in *L'Invitation au château,* Colombe in

17

*Colombe* and Lucile in *La Répétition* all could be called *invitées au château.*[3]

These twenty-year-old *invitées* possess unusual powers. They can relieve their partners' sorrows and longings, provide them with safe islands of escape and inspire in them hopes for a happy future. The most complete description of Anouilh's young female redeemer appears in *La Répétition*. The exemplary Anouilhesque heroine follows this pattern:

> She's not romantic, she's tender. She's not naive, she's good. She's not hard, she's direct . . . She's alone, radiant and naked under her little cotton dress. (376)

In the *Pièces roses,* Anouilh confronts us with more young lovers. Gustave and Juliette in *Le Bal des voleurs* are in harmony with the world and for them alone the comedy turns into success, because they have played it with all the zest of youth "and only because they were playing their youth, a thing which always succeeds. They were not even aware of the comedy" (130). By the end of the play, they leave the stage hand in hand, with a promising future lying ahead of them. In *Le Rendez-vous de Senlis,* we have an identical situation; by the end of the play, Isabelle proves strong enough to lead Georges over all the environmental hurdles toward a future full of hope.

The third hero in the *Pièces roses* who is saved by a young girl is the Prince in *Léocadia* who earlier in his life experienced three unforgettable days with Léocadia, an extravagant woman who strangled herself with a scarf, involuntarily it seems.[4] Since then he has refused to acknowledge time's victory over those three days and lives surrounded by people who in one way or another witnessed his short-lived happiness. When street urchins run after him, jeering at his folly, the Prince finds an easy refuge in the castle garden behind the walls encircling his aunt's property. There, among those who have been hired to foster his dreams,[5] he can forget the *others*, a luxury not granted the heroes of the *Pièces noires*. The Prince finally is saved by Amanda, the young *invitée* who is stronger than nostalgia because she is hope. She makes him forget Léocadia by becoming a new Léocadia for him, and—most likely—a source of future regrets.

Love is triumphant in the *Pièces roses*, and the pervading optimistic point of view suggests that a person can be saved by another person. Anouilh was between nineteen and twenty-nine years old when he wrote his *Pièces roses*, and if there is hope in these early plays, it is because he focuses on young lovers, whereas the aging characters, who incarnate the *noir*, are given roles of secondary importance.

When Anouilh wrote his *Pièces brillantes*, he was older, between thirty-seven and forty years old, like Héro and Tigre in *La Répétition ou L'Amour puni*. *L'Amour puni* could serve as an epigraph for the whole collection of *Pièces brillantes*. To be sure, the young girls "bright and clean in their little cotton dresses" reappear, but they are no longer so strong and firm as in the *Pièces roses*. Their partners have aged too and are burdened with the fatigue of life.

The innocent flower girl Colombe cannot resist the lure of the theatre. Taken from her own pure world and exposed to that of the *château*, Lucile succumbs to its frivolous atmosphere. Julien's consolation for having lost Colombe lies in his memories of their first meeting, whereas Héro ends *La Répétition* by calling out the name of the girl of his lost dream: Evangeline! In contrast to the *Pièces roses*, in which nostalgia is overcome by hope, in the *Pièces brillantes* hope is crushed and ground into nostalgia, a process that reaches its climax in the *Pièces grinçantes.*

A power stronger than love makes itself felt in the *Pièces brillantes,* one against which love is helpless: time. In the castle everyone lives "as if no one knew," but beneath the shiny veneer the invisible enemy lurks. When Héro says to Tigre, "You seem depressed," and asks "How old are you?" (417) its presence can be felt. As Anouilh's heroes grow older, their nostalgia becomes keener. However, at the noon-tide of the *Pièces brillantes,* when they, like Anouilh, are only thirty-seven, there is still some hope. "He'll be sad for a month or two—then he'll start playing again" (477), says Tigre's wife, alluding to Tigre's despair on account of Lucile's departure.

At curtain fall, the young *invitées* have been hurt, and the love seekers, having pursued a dream in vain, must content themselves with a sigh of regret or take refuge in the cult of a single moment of beauty already buried in the past. The question at the end of *Le Rendez-vous de Senlis*—How long will they be happy?—becomes at the end of *La Répétition:* How long will they be able to play the game?

In two of the *Pièces grinçantes, Ardèle* and *La Valse des toréadors,* Anouilh's love seekers have progressed further on the curve of time along which they are traveling. Anouilh now centers his plays on aging couples; the young are relegated to secondary roles. After seventeen years of mar-riage, General Saint-Pé is still dreaming of his "Léocadia," Mademoiselle de Sainte-Euverte, with whom he danced an unforgettable waltz seventeen years earlier at a military ball at Saumur. In all the years he has spent at the side of his hated and hateful wife, *la générale,* Saint-Pé has never

stopped thinking about the young girl from the Saumur
dance floor. Miraculously, after seventeen years, Mademoiselle de Sainte-Euverte arrives at the General's home, only to
throw herself into the arms of Saint-Pé's young secretary
Gaston. The General's dream of lasting love, confronted with
its embodiment seventeen years later, crumbles to pieces, and
Saint-Pé is left with the sole consolation of pinching the new
maid, Pamela. As he approaches the end of his life, his dream
has shrunk to the size of this gesture, and time is so precious
that he cannot afford to lose a single minute on hope or
regret. Time is definitely the enemy of love. The greater the
intensity of love, the greater the final solitude; the more
desperate the nostalgia, the heavier the fall from hope. In the
end all that remains of Léocadia is a scarf; of love, in the final
analysis, probably no more than pinching Pamela. "Don't
think about me, ever. Don't ever think about love" (82).
These two sentences from *Ardèle* seem to express Anouilh's
final verdict at the end of his trial of love.

The Prince, Julien, Héro and Saint-Pé are rebels against
time. Each of them has known a fleeting moment of great
happiness and all refuse to admit that it is in the nature of
things that happiness be fleeting. Héro is haunted by the
memory of a girl who has died, with whom he was in love
eighteen years earlier and whom he would have married had
not his friend Tigre intervened and persuaded him that the
girl was an unsuitable choice. Héro cannot forget Evangeline,
and still, after eighteen years of dissipation and addiction to
alcohol, he cherishes her memory as if she were a saint. Had
he only married her, they could have been happy together
and the girl spared her sorrow. Yet, as a critic sensibly
advances, seen in the perspective of Anouilh's entire theatre,
there is an ironic twist to Héro's adulation of Evangeline's

memory, for it is precisely because Tigre "prevented him from marrying her that Evangeline can still symbolize ideal love for Héro."[6] For love cannot afford permanence. The Amandas of this world, just like the Léocadias, cannot possibly give their Princes more than "three days" of happiness, more than "those twenty-four hours, that pitiful little day" that life, according to M. Henri in *Eurydice* (487) holds in store for young lovers. Those who blind themselves to this basic truth about love, seeking in love a little "eternity," a reason for which to live, a weapon against the absurd, are inevitably deceived and, for so long as they persist, are condemned to move within an endless cycle of hope and regret.

Not only are "three days" of happiness all that time can spare young lovers, but even these "three days" may pass them by entirely. In *L'Invitation au château,* the unknowing slaves to love's chimera would probably go on forever pursuing the wrong partner, were it not for the appearance of the young *invitée* Isabelle and for the wisdom of the old chatelaine Mme Desmermortes who takes the amorous affairs of her two nephews in hand just in time to provide the play's happy ending. "All we love is our own love, my children, and we run all our life after this small, fleeting image of ourselves," says Mme Desmermortes to the young novices in love. But fortunately there are "a few old ladies who have given up this folly and who have begun to see clearly, at the time, alas, when one needs to put on glasses" (145).

In the *Pièces roses* and *Pièces brillantes,* the stanchest advocates of compromise in love and in life are three old ladies: Lady Hurf in *Le Bal des voleurs,* the Duchess in *Léocadia* and Mme Desmermortes in *L'Invitation au château.*

In the last tableau of *Léocadia,* in a section of the castle's park where the Prince finally forgets Léocadia in Amanda's

arms, shots can be heard in the distance. The Duchess and her
ridiculous escort Hector are passing their time shooting birds.
In the last scene of this tableau, the game-keeper appears on
stage carrying something in his game-bag. A bird has been
shot down. An extravagant, outlandish bird, the game-keeper
keeps explaining:

> A strange bird. Its feathers are too long, it falls in traps
> wherever it goes, its feet are so long it doesn't fit
> anywhere. And on top of everything, with those bright
> feathers it can be spotted miles away. (372-73)

This strange, very vulnerable and awkward bird appears as
the symbol of Léocadia, the symbol of the futile dream of
love that, according to the Duchess, must be cast away at all
cost in order that everybody may breathe freely again and
resume the journey through life at a normal pace. At the
mercy of time, love, like life itself, carries the seed of its own
destruction. It gives itself away like the bright-colored bird,
its feathers much too long and its squawk all too loud. It
destroys itself like Léocadia with her own scarf.

The bird must be shot down so that the Prince may live;
yet once it is shot down, the Duchess is the first to pay
modest tribute to Léocadia in words that can be taken as a
charming, although ironical epitaph to love:

> But as useless, frivolous and basically unjust as this
> poor, dear outlandish creature may have seemed, no one
> can prevent us from shedding a little tear in remem-
> brance of her. (374)

As for the bird, the Duchess orders that it be buried, with
all due respect to its frivolous beauty, in her rose garden.

The bird is also shot down symbolically in *La Répétition*

as Héro seduces Lucile after overcoming her resistance with a
skillfully contrived lie about Tigre to whom Lucile has given
herself the previous night in true love. The presence of true
love in their midst appears intolerable to the inhabitants of
the castle's corrupt and cynical universe. After Lucile's departure everything is restored to order once more, with the
exception of Héro who, having acquitted himself of a job
well done chooses to die in a duel rather than go on living a
life which, after the first betrayal, calls for a never ending
succession of self-delusions, lies and new betrayals. He is the
real hero of *La Répétition* and Anouilh's most tragic rebel
against time. Through him, Anouilh, very much in the tradition of the poet Laforgue, deflates the romantic myth for
which, in the same breath, he voices craving and nostalgia.
Héro kills the bird, but with tears running down his face.
"My child. My sweet child. My poor little lost waif" (464),
he cajoles Lucile as the girl sinks back, no longer resisting
him, ready to embark on the path of life without a dream.

In the *Pièces roses*, *Pièces brillantes* and two of the *Pièces
grinçantes*, the value of love is weighed against the universal
background of time. In the *Pièces noires* and *Nouvelles Pièces
noires*, written during the same period, the value of love is
examined within the much narrower perspective of an im-
mediate environment, not as a plea for permanence, but
rather as a plea for understanding.

Families, I hate you!

(Gide, *Les Nourritures terrestres*)

During our lifetime, there live on our planet some three to four billion people—among them, there are five perfect partners for each of us and some five hundred compatible ones. The rest . . .

(From a computer-based news item)

## 3. REBELLION AGAINST ENVIRONMENT: PIÈCES NOIRES

In the *Pièces noires,*[1] in contrast to the *Pièces roses* and *Pièces brillantes,* Anouilh's characters function in the midst of life's turmoil. More often than not, we are introduced into milieus where poverty is prevalent. This is true of the setting in the first act of *La Sauvage* where a bandstand occupies the better part of the stage, arranged to represent the interior of a seaside resort café. In the first act of *Eurydice,* we see a refreshment room in a provincial railway station. In the second and fourth acts of *Eurydice,* the characters are in a big, somber, dirty room in a provincial hotel; in the three acts of *Jézabel,* in the room of an impoverished young man. Even in the bourgeois home of the father of Julia, Jeannette and Lucien in *Roméo et Jeannette,* the accent is on shabbiness; the action in Acts I, II and IV of *Roméo et Jeannette* takes place in a large, badly furnished room in a sprawling, dilapidated house.[2]

This is the type of setting in which Anouilh places his young lovers: Florent and Thérèse in *La Sauvage,* Frantz and

25

Monime in *L'Hermine,* Marc and Jacqueline in *Jézabel,*
Frédéric and Jeannette in *Roméo et Jeannette* and Orpheus*
and Eurydice in *Eurydice.* With the exception of Orpheus
and Eurydice, who are both poor, the lovers in the *Pièces
noires* belong to different social classes. One partner is rich,
the other poor, and it is always the poor one who is seeking
perfection in love, dreaming of finding an absolute in love,
hoping to be completely understood by his partner.

The twenty-year-old working-class girl in her cheap cotton dress reappears in the *Pièces noires,* but here, from the
very outset, she lacks the innocence of her counterpart in the
*Pièces roses* and *Pièces brillantes.* Thérèse, Jeannette and
Eurydice, all are deeply marked by their environments. At
the time of their meetings with their ideal partners, these girls
have already acquired burdensome pasts, filled with events
which they would rather forget. But struggle as they may,
with themselves and against others, Thérèse, Jeannette and
Eurydice are unable to forget their memories of the past: it
weighs upon the present and intensifies their search for a
different way of life. Each in his own way, Marc, Frantz,
Thérèse, Eurydice and Jeannette finds himself engulfed in the
squalor of an environment inhabited by three distinct cate-
gories of people who constitute Anouilh's stage humanity:
the mediocre race, the compromisers and the heroes. The
definition of the mediocre race and the heroes is given in
*Eurydice* by M. Henri:

> There are two races of men. One race, large in number,
> forever multiplying, submissive—a hamburger-eating race

*The original French spelling of the names of characters in Anouilh's
plays has been retained throughout the book except in the case of
famous historical or legendary figures such as Joan of Arc, Napoleon,
Creon and Orpheus when the English spelling is used.

dutifully producing its offspring, working hard, saving money, year after year, through epidemics and wars, on and on; people made to live, everyday people, people one can hardly imagine dead. And then there are the heroes. Those one can well imagine lying on the floor, face white, shot, blood dripping from a fresh wound, one moment triumphant with an honor guard—next flanked by two policemen. (470)

The most distinctive representatives of the mediocre race in the *Pièces noires,* are the parents whom Anouilh depicts as having been reduced by life to the last dregs of humanity, to one-dimensionality; mechanisms reacting to stimuli in an almost animal-like manner. Seemingly unaware of the freedom of choice, they accept without questioning whatever comes their way. They are machines for eating, drinking, belching, penny-squeezing and fornicating. An occasional infidelity and from time to time chicken Italian-style with Armagnac is all the father in *La Sauvage* asks of life. His language abounds with clichés and vulgarisms. At the table he hiccups and scratches himself, shedding dandruff into his food. His subjection to money is pathological. While a taxicab waits outside he can hardly speak: he seems umbilically tied to the taximeter; a spasm of pain runs through him whenever he senses that the fatal money machine outside is registering a new unit.

The parents in *La Sauvage* are orchestra players, tied to their instruments by their need for a means of survival. The orchestra symbolizes the degradation of men reduced to the status of mere pegs in the wheel of economic necessity. Anouilh's orchestra players are like so many chorus voices, living reminders of an everpresent mediocre reality from which the heroes of the *Pièces noires* are trying to break loose.

The mothers and fathers in the *Pièces noires* are *ugly parents.* The mother in *Jézabel* goes from one infidelity to the next, drinks heavily and begs her husband for money to prevent her latest and possibly last lover from leaving her. The fathers in *Eurydice* and *Roméo et Jeannette* cannot grasp anything going on outside their little worlds. Confronted by tragedies unfolding in spheres totally alien to them, all they can do is sit back in wonderment, puffing on cigars, uttering platitudes.

The compromisers in the *Pièces noires* are a different category of stage characters. They are clearsighted and sensitive enough to perceive the two sides of the game being played. They are an in-between species, neither mediocre nor heroic. They understand both the sordid condition of the mediocre race and the plight of the heroes. They might have been heroes themselves had they been cut out for a big role. However, they never had the courage to take the first step. So they have become the eternal arguers, philosopher-friends, advisers, intelligent wits, ironical toward themselves, often cynical and resigned. They see clearly but do not know how to, or do not dare or simply refuse to live in the light of this clarity. Such is Frantz's friend Philippe in *L'Hermine,* Florent's friend Hartman in *La Sauvage,* Jeannette's brother Lucien in *Roméo et Jeannette* and M. Henri in *Eurydice.*

Marc, Thérèse, Orpheus and Jeannette are the most prominent heroes in the *Pièces noires,* characters who in spite of the downward pull of their environments have preserved deep inside a more consummate humaneness, a pure mind capable of irrational impulses. For a long time they have been waiting for a partner who would fully share their irrational cravings. And with the exception of Gaston in *Le Voyageur sans bagage* each of them has been fortunate enough to meet such a person. Marc has found his Jacqueline, Frantz his

Monime, Thérèse her Florent, Orpheus his Eurydice and Jeannette her Frédéric. Through these couples of lovers, Anouilh illustrates his version of the myth of the Androgyne: the search by each severed part of a once perfect, whole being for its lost counterpart, a search rewarded perhaps once in every century.

Anouilh judges reality from the height of the ideal and inevitably, seen from high up, the world seems a very sad place to live. At the same time, in showing reality in black coloring, Anouilh places the ideal into proper perspective. Confronted with hopes rising from the lowest depths, the true value of the myth can be better determined. From the outset of a *Pièce noire* it is evident that, as in the tragedies of antiquity, the heroes in search of absolutes will not be able to master their fates. It is not for nothing that the Greek gods decided to divide the enormous strength of the Androgyne. They could not tolerate anything on earth that would equal their power, and they considered two creatures perfectly matched a dangerous threat to their supremacy.

Creation negates those who strive to equal her. The heroes must respect certain limits; in stepping over them they negate the human community and the gods who watch over it. A certain tension in moderation is the most that can be tolerated; beyond that the wrong path begins and whoever takes it commits a crime for which the inevitable punishment, if not death, is a severe reduction in power. To argue like Camus' Caligula that it is often necessary to take the wrong path in order to be able to know with any amount of assurance that it is indeed the wrong one seems a very dubious justification and consolation. Particularly when, as in the case of the Androgyne seekers in Anouilh's *Pièces noires,* we find ourselves embarked with the heroes on the frivolous path of love. Lucien advising Frédéric not to be taken in by love for the Fellow Up There doesn't care for love at all, argues in favor of the humble line of compromise:

> Marry Julia. Have children. Become a man. A man with a profession, a man with money, a man with a mistress. Nobody'll mind that. Be a real man. Don't play around with fate. It's so easy to be happy! There are formulas, and men have spent centuries perfecting them. Cheat, my dear; don't take anything seriously, least of all yourself. It's the only way to live in peace with That Fellow Up Above. He has a soft spot for cheaters or else he is shortsighted, or perhaps asleep ... And if you don't make too much noise chances are he won't interfere ... But he's got a nose, a phenomenal sense of smell and a whiff, the slightest whiff of love, it gets to him. And he doesn't like it, not a bit. He's allergic to love. It wakes him up and before you know it he's down on you. All hell breaks lose. You are twisted around, like in the army. Left. Right. Up. Down. Until you die. (279)

But the wisdom of the clearsighted arguers has no impact on the heroes who blindly, following their irrational impulses are bound to discover the rules of the game only after much hurtful experience. The adviser's role in the *Pièces noires* coincides therefore with that of a detached observer who watches the hero slowly move toward his undoing. Wise like Death whose spokesman he appears to be, M. Henri knows what the future holds in store for the heroes. Lucien very much resembles him, knowledgeable as he is about the habits of God. Hartman is more modest but he too is clearsighted to the point at which he can no longer be taken by surprise. These characters are lucid intellectuals who clearly see the *yes* and *no* of each argument and comment with a mixture of amusement and sadness on the predicament of human beings lost and abandoned between two infinites.

If the decor and angle of observation in the *Pièces noires* differs from those in the *Pièces roses, Pièces brillantes* and two of the *Pièces grinçantes,* the basic idea inherent in the plays in both these groups is the same: He who commits all his hopes and desires to Love must sooner or later dearly pay for such poor judgment. In the *Pièces roses, Pièces brillantes* and two of the *Pièces grinçantes,* Anouilh insists more on what time does to love. In the *Pièces noires* he shows to what extent love itself appears to be love's worst enemy. His heroes in these plays place love too high, as if, compelled by some masochistic urge, they want its failure.

Mythology and even history have provided us with a few love stories of exceptional beauty; Anouilh is attracted to them for they afford him with the opportunity to strike out for the Ideal as well as to castigate the world for not living up to it. In *Roméo et Jeannette* Lucien speaks of a woman with whom a dreamer might possibly establish an Androgyne. This woman, the wife of Poetus, a Roman condemned to death by Nero, is shown on an engraving and Lucien interprets the scene:

> She just snatched the sword from the centurion's hand and, while Poetus stood hesitating, she first stabbed herself—then offering the sword to her husband, she said smiling: Here, it doesn't hurt. (306)

Cynical and undeceived, Lucien cannot help but disparage what deep inside he still cherishes and craves for:

> First Empire style, you know. She wasn't very beautiful, the wife of Poetus, perhaps a bit heavy in contour for

delicate fellows as ourselves. Nonetheless ... (he sighs, half dreamingly, half mockingly) Lucky Poetus! (307)

When Jeannette wants to know whether there has ever been a single woman who has loved with all her might and forever, Lucien says: "I've never had her number" (312), while tacitly admitting that it may very well be that Poetus' wife truly loved. The same is true for the Androgyne. It is very much possible that somewhere she exists, but nobody in the *Pièces noires* knows where.

The heroes in the *Pièces noires* are deaf to arguments in favor of a humble sort of happiness. They want all or nothing at all, and the lower they stand, the greater their claims on the Ideal, the louder their plea for help from the companion meant to share it. As Thérèse, Orpheus and Jeannette rebel against their environments with growing impatience, they become more demanding of their partners. To conform with their idea of the perfect couple, their partners ultimately would have to become simple extensions of the hero himself. Because Florent, Eurydice and Frédéric are *other,* products of their own pasts, fashioned by their own environments, they can never fully respond to the yearnings of Thérèse, Orpheus and Jeannette, unable to save them from their thirst for the absolute.

Thérèse finds Florent too distant, easygoing and kind. When Hartman reminds her that even so Florent may well be her true redeemer, Thérèse refuses a redemption that would be soft. She dreams of a hard and cruel redeemer who would have had the same experiences as she herself and thus be able to understand completely her every mood and urge.[3] Like Marc in *Jézabel,* Thérèse is dominated by her past and tainted by her environment. Thérèse runs away from her chance for redemption. She leaves under the benevolent gaze of Hartman who foresees that with such an attitude toward life, Thérèse is bound to run into all the sharp corners of the world.

Eurydice abandons Orpheus, feeling that with the kind of past she has had she could never match his high expectations. Jeannette leaves to rejoin and eventually marry her old lover because of Frédéric's inability to sacrifice everything to their love: at the news of his fiancée's suicide he rushes away, at the very moment when Jeannette most needs him and when to her mind he should have been able to forget the entire world for the sake of their love.

In pursuing the quest of the Androgyne to the limits of the visible world, Orpheus discovers that whatever one does, two can never truly become one and that consequently one is always alone, each a prisoner of his own bag of skin. Only in death will he be able to establish a perfect union with Eurydice. Jeannette and Frédéric also find life a source of inevitable discord and only when close to death, as they wait at the end of the play for the rising tide to engulf them, do they begin to form the Androgyne.

In *Eurydice* and *Roméo et Jeannette,* the deaths of the lovers follow the storyline underlying the legends. In the other *Pièces noires,* where he does not have the easy mythical excuse for disposing of his lovers in such an old-fashioned way, Anouilh has his seekers of a better world leave the stage shortly before the final curtainfall. This is the case with Thérèse, Marc, Lucien and also with Gaston in *Le Voyageur sans bagage.*

For Thérèse and to a lesser degree for Marc and Gaston, departure means the beginning of a new quest. Robert Kemp, wondering what the future may well hold for Thérèse, con-

cludes that she is bound to become a saint, alluding to the
fact that only by accepting new obligations can Thérèse find
real emancipation.[4] Seen in the perspective of his entire
theatre, the kind of obligation Anouilh had in mind for
Thérèse becomes apparent in *Antigone,* written eight years
after *La Sauvage.*

Antigone begins where Thérèse stops. Thérèse rejects
marriage as the answer to her aspirations at the end of the
play; Antigone, right from the beginning. Thérèse's hope of
discovering "a white clearing at the farthest end of despair
where one is almost happy" (261) becomes "dirty hope" in
*Antigone.* Antigone refuses hope as such. She cannot exercise
freedom unless she is free of hope.

In anticipating the gift of grace, Thérèse resigns herself to
the verdict of eternal law and finds nothing on her path but
God's implacable silence. Antigone, challenging justice, acts
within the confines of temporal law and encounters opposition in the form of a representative of this law, Creon. For
Thérèse, grace is a goal; for Antigone, a result. Thérèse seeks
an absolute value in a form as deceptive as that of man;
Antigone avoids the risk of being deceived by identifying
herself, not with a man, but with a cause. Thérèse's protest
against God's silence is lost in a vacuum, since there is no one
to intercept her one-sided dialogue with the eternal; Antigone
fulfills herself from one moment to the next, along with the
cause she defends.

In *Antigone* and *L'Alouette,* Anouilh takes his twenty-
year-old girls from mythology and history. Attracted to the
exceptional, he found in Antigone and in Joan of Arc two of
the clearest and most touching figures of mankind that have
braved authority in the name of personal conviction. In
making these two voices echo his own innermost voice,
Anouilh wrote his two clearest and most touching plays.

> As long as the kingdom of justice and freedom
> is not established on the earth it is necessary
> that voices be heard which are capable of awak-
> ening humanity lost in sleep.
>
> (Abellio)

## 4. REBELLION FOR A CAUSE:
### *ANTIGONE, L'ALOUETTE* AND *BECKET*

In *Antigone* and *L'Alouette* a new philosophical dimen-
sion makes itself felt in Anouilh's theatre. Parallel with the
deepening of philosophical content, we find a change in the
plays' settings to suggest an expansion from the local to the
universal. The scene shifts from the stifling bourgeois interi-
ors, maids' rooms, cheap hotel rooms, castle drawing rooms,
refreshment counters in provincial stations and parks at
health resorts. Anouilh's characters have exchanged these
shut-in private family worlds for the broader and more neu-
tral settings of *Antigone* and *L'Alouette* and the historical
backgrounds of the royal palaces of *Becket* and *La Foire
d'Empoigne*. At the same time, Anouilh adds characters to
each of his three fundamental groups: the mediocre race, the
compromisers and the heroes.

In *Antigone*, mediocrity is incarnated in the guards Jonas,
Boudousse, and Durand. Having delivered Antigone to Creon,
the guards expect double pay and discuss raptuously the way
they will spend it without their wives' knowledge. No tragedy
can affect the Boudousses of this world who are here to do
their work and draw their salaries. They serve the powers that
be, and should the devil himself seize power one day, they

35

will serve him faithfully. Boudousse may indeed be "immortal." Two millenia elapse between Antigone's rebellion in mythological Greece and the rebellion of Joan of Arc in medieval France, but Boudousse ironically reappears in *L'Alouette*.

In *Antigone, L'Alouette* and *Pauvre Bitos,* Anouilh applies the term *mediocre* to a much broader segment of humanity than, for example, in *La Sauvage*. Although the *ugly parents* are present in *L'Alouette,* they are not isolated units like the families in *La Sauvage* but archipelagos in the vast sea of mediocrity referred to in *Antigone* as *the crowd,* a conglomerate of everyday people, an indeterminate clay-like mass of human flesh. The characteristics of the crowd are extreme opportunism, short memory and an acute need to turn in the direction in which the wind is blowing. In her days of triumph the crowd followed Joan, only to turn away from her in her hours of defeat. On the day scheduled for Joan's execution the crowd starts gathering around the stake at early dawn, fighting for good seats to watch the burning. It is the same crowd that would have hailed Joan enthusiastically had she taken Rouen.

Anouilh has accentuated the non-thinking side of the members of the mediocre race in a number of individual characterizations. For instance Beaudricourt in *L'Alouette* never has had an idea of his own. When he is not sleeping, eating, playing games or making love, when he is not touching, seeing, smelling, tasting or hearing, it is as if he did not exist; he feels lost in a total void. Jonas, Boudousse and Durand secrete something inhuman. Their minds and feelings are not sufficiently developed to enable them to grasp the absurd. Like all other injustices from which they are free, the absurd does not interest them. Functioning on an almost vegetal level, the mediocre ones are not capable to arriving at a conclusion based on judgment; their actions are not the result of free choice. They are unaware that beyond the common everyday life lies the heroic domain, based on lucid vision and intelligence, which takes into account a vast amount of experience and suffering. However, between the "hell" of mediocrity and the artificial paradise of heroism stretches the vast territory of compromise.

Without exception, all the compromisers in Anouilh's theatre regard ideals as children's diseases which must be overcome early in life, like measles or smallpox. Life's veterans in Anouilh's plays watch the awkward heroes with amusement, tenderness and chagrin, referring to them as *mon petit* or *mon enfant*. From the heights of their experience they repeat that life is not what the heroes playing with knives, pistols, shovels or banners think it is. Creon urges Antigone to get plump, marry and have children. With babies crying in the house, according to the Inquisitor in *L'Alouette,* there will be no danger of Joan's hearing other voices, particularly those likely to cause disturbance to the state and church.

The compromisers constitute the world of "yes" sayers, a world referred to in *Antigone* as *the kitchen,* in which truth is no more than a lie repeated often enough; justice, a synonym for injustice; sincerity, a form of strategy like any other; and honor, an outdated proposition advanced only by a few troubled die-hards. Self-interest governs all human actions and a number of remarks uttered by Anouilh's compromisers sound as if taken directly from La Rochefoucauld's *Maximes.* Anouilh presents the political kitchen, in which his compromisers are cast as the chief cooks, as a frightening mechanism for organized murder in charge of tracking down the kitchen's worst enemy: the insolent man who says "no."

It is a world in which every man is out for himself, where the winner takes all and where idealism is most definitely not the proper sort of luggage for life.

Certain compromisers in Anouilh's historical and mythological plays play parts from history's vast repertory; those who inspired their roles are dead: masks, statues, myths, life summaries in encyclopedias, pictures in school books. Anouilh has chosen some of these figures from the Grand Guignol of history and mythology, re-interpreted certain highlights from their lives and called upon professional actors to animate their masks. The compromisers are in varying degrees conscious that they are playing roles. Some of them play them with utter seriousness and conviction, as if God himself had let them in on the secret of his creation. They speak with disconcerting finality. Others show more awareness that they are playing parts, yet this cynical knowledge by no means detracts from their enjoyment of the game. Creon is an exception among Anouilh's compromisers. He understands the implications of his role to the extent that, at times, he seems reluctant to continue playing it. The role forces him to act against his heart's desire; he would like to save Antigone, yet he must send her to death; personally, he feels inclined to dispose of Polynices' body in the same decorous way as Eteocles', but the interests of state oblige him to act otherwise.

In Creon, the human being and the mask are more at odds than in any other compromiser. Creon is ill suited for his part—yet, his grandeur is due precisely to the disunity of the person and the persona. Anouilh shows us a Creon who has not been able to develop that certain liking for his role apparent in the characterization of Louis XVIII in *La Foire d'Empoigne,* without speaking of the total identification of the person with the role in the case of Anouilh's Napoleon. To point out how much of a character's spontaneous ego must be silenced for the sake of pretense, Anouilh has put into Creon's mouth the most tragic words pronounced by a compromiser on his stage: "Nothing is true except what one keeps to himself" (186).

Creon favors the simple, everyday happiness of ordinary people to the sublime, half-demented happiness sometimes attained by those who seek absolutes, reached at the very end of a long road of suffering. A sweet home, a happy couple with children, surrounded by familiar objects to provide them with shelter from the mad, unpredictable face of the absurd—such is Creon's ideal of happiness elaborated through the course of years of experience and in the process of growing old. In Creon's world there exists only the reality understood by reason. To uphold and impose upon others a rational universe, Creon relies on the law, a police force established with the purpose of maintaining this law, and a social hierarchy expected to abide by it. The concern with seeming by far dominates the need for being. Creon may not believe in the formulae spoken by the Theban priests—yet he considers all such pretenses necessary in the public interest. Anouilh's compromisers are characters who have ceased to live their lives spontaneously. They incarnate in varying degrees the loss of a deeper humanity; they are human beings turned into conventional masks. The most despicable among them, like the Promoter and the Inquisitor in *L'Alouette,* are so thoroughly identified with their masks that they are no longer aware of playing roles.

Creon goes through the outer motions of his role, yet in doing so he suffers. He plays his role in the rational city of men yet he cannot dismiss the other side of the coin with a simple shrug. He feels a secret admiration for Antigone's attitude toward the absurd, a feeling mixed with a certain amount of envy. If only it were possible for childhood never to end, if only one could postpone indefinitely the time of choosing. Creon manifests a deep appreciation and nostalgia for the irresponsible days of childhood, but once embarked on the path away from the absurd he can no longer afford the luxury of giving in to his most private feelings. A step further and he too could wind up in denunciation of the universal order of things. Instead, he silences the voice of his heart and at the play's end he leaves to attend a committee meeting.

The heroic attitude toward the absurd presupposes a conception of reality split into the rational and the intuitive. Anouilh's Antigone alludes to this intuitive super-reality when telling Creon in the course of their debate that she speaks to him from a kingdom from which he with his wrinkles, his wisdom and big stomach stands excluded. She refuses to come to terms with Creon's common everyday reality, rejecting *a priori* Creon's reasonable arguments.

If it is impossible for reason to clarify everything and thereby attain absolute unity by abolishing the *absurd walls,* then all rational systems can be but relative. Thus, a step further after the realization of the mind's limitations, and there comes the revelation of the relativity of truth, an important discovery for Anouilh's hero who opposes his own truth to an old established one that takes itself all too seriously. Anouilh uses the relativity-of-truth conception as a powerful instrument of social critique, ridiculing through his heroes the blind, pretentious reason that claims that everything is clear. Antigone's voice in opposition to Creon's rational universe is that of a child boldly proclaiming that the king is naked.

In *Antigone,* Anouilh glorifies the childhood years, con-
trasting their purity and innocence with the compromises of
age. Ideally, Antigone would like for childhood to go on
indefinitely. Beyond childhood, she finds the certitude she
demands of life only in total identification with the cause she
has chosen to defend: the burial of her brother's uncovered
body. In her rebellion, Antigone prolongs her childhood; in
death, she crowns it with an aura of eternity.

A child's weapon stands out in the play as a touching
symbol of the heroine's rebellion; to cover her brother's body
with earth, Antigone uses the same shovel which she used
when she was a little girl building sand castles on the beach.
Another object that is suggestive of a child's universe is the
paper flower Polynices once gave to her. She has kept it like a
sacred relic, and on the morning of her fatal decision she
sought in its sight the necessary courage to leave her room
and go bury the uninterred body.

In *L'Alouette,* Anouilh likewise exalts childhood and
early youth. Joan, the "Christian Antigone,"[1] wants the
story of her life to begin with a scene in her father's house,
when she was still a little girl, at the time she was tending
sheep in the fields, when the Voices addressed her for the
first time.

Both Joan and Antigone have sudden revelations concerning duties to be performed. Antigone must bury the uninterred body of Polynices which lies exposed to vultures; Joan
must save the Kingdom of France from the exposure to the
abuse of the English soldiers. Their heroic acts having been
accomplished, both are being judged as enemies of the established order. They express identical views on courage, have
the same horror of old age and, at about the same stage in the
development of the two plays, experience a moment of
doubt. Antigone agrees to repudiate her cause after Creon has

shown her that Polynices was far from the ideal brother she thought he was. Joan signs the act of renunciation when she realizes that all her friends have deserted her. Ultimately, both heroines withdraw their renunciations and reaffirm their rebellions. They refuse to accept the trite everyday happiness described by Creon and Warwick as the only possible way of life.

The endings of both *Antigone* and *L'Alouette* are ironical as in both cases the stage is occupied by representatives of the mediocre race. In *Antigone* the last image seen by the spectator is that of the guards playing cards. The last words in *L'Alouette* are spoken by Joan's father, who used to break sticks on his daughter's back to teach her to be reasonable and who appears just before curtain fall to claim a share of Joan's posthumous glory for himself.[2]

Antigone and Joan remain Anouilh's purest and most cherished heroines, in whom he glorifies intuition at the expense of reason and scientific investigation. Discussing Joan of Arc as a historical figure, Anouilh ridicules the scholar intent on explaining the irrational aspects of Joan's rebellion in the light of the social and political forces in action in France at the beginning of the fifteenth century.

> You cannot explain Joan, any more than you can explain the tiniest flower growing by the wayside. There's just a little living flower that has always known, ever since it was a microscopic seed, how many petals it would have and how big they would grow, exactly how blue its blue would be and how its delicate scent would be compounded. There's just the phenomenon of Joan, as there is the phenomenon of a daisy or of the sky or of a bird. What pretentious creatures men are, if that's not enough for them.[3]

Books describe Joan as a big, healthy girl, but Anouilh cannot care less. He sees her *skinny* like Antigone, a strangely stubborn, undernourished little girl, who, at her trial, knew how to undermine the dialectics of seventy judges in their stiff robes with a single, simple little answer. He exalts the young girl's faith in her cause which proved stronger than the rational edifice of the military strategists and the political experts of her time.

The "shooting of the bird" in *Antigone* and *L'Alouette* is more spectacular than in *Léocadia* or *La Répétition* because it involves the larger community of men and not only private castle worlds. Antigone's and Joan's rebellions are based on exalted heroic will rather than private feelings. For Antigone and Joan freedom means above all the freedom to choose their own deaths. A true hero is his own father: he needs no one but himself to accomplish his design; he dies when he wants to, as he pleases, from the cause he wills. He can master his fate by *obliging* others to kill him when he so chooses rather than live at the mercy of an untimely death or in perpetual danger of the loss of a dream. Yet, the supreme stage manager, God, has distributed only a very limited number of such great heroic roles. Not all heroes have been honored like Antigone and Joan with trials and grandiose executions favoring their later day legends.

After *Antigone* and *L'Alouette*, *Becket* provided Anouilh with a new opportunity to exalt a person chosen for the fulfillment of a mission. In four acts and twenty-seven tableaux, Anouilh carries us through sixteen years of Becket's life, from the time that Becket became Henry's Chancellor at the age of thirty-six to the day of his murder in the cathedral at the age of fifty-two.[4]

From the moment the curtain rises, Becket behaves like a

man who is familiar with the extent of nature's and man's indifference toward man. For him, trees, flowers and blades of grass have long since lost the luster they have for Antigone and Joan at the outset of their rebellions. Becket is a person who has already experienced the moment of truth which, as Camus points out in *Le Mythe de Sisyphe,* is likely to steal into life at about the age of thirty, bringing with it the revelation of the absurd.

To counteract the absurd, Becket identifies with his role. He is willing to play whatever part he is given and to play it as best he can. "One has to gamble with one's life in order to feel alive" (163), he says. As the king's companion in pleasure, he applies himself to his task so well that he succeeds in outwenching the king himself, who is fifteen years his junior. As Chancellor of England, he serves the state with utmost zeal. He accepts the honor bestowed upon him with the following words: "My Lord and King has given me his Seal with the Three Lions to keep. My mother is England now" (160). And when the king finally makes him Archbishop of Canterbury he once again proves himself a most faithful servant, not the king's, however, but God's.

Anouilh traces Becket's evolution through his various roles. All the time—while brilliantly playing the role of Henry's companion and counselor, while saying the right words and making the proper gestures to conform to the political expedients of the moment—deep within himself, he preserves a firm sense of honor. In the absence of a noble cause with which to identify, Becket is obliged to improvise his honor for many years. And he would have never discovered it had not the role of archbishop suddenly been entrusted to him. Made into God's servant, Becket's honor becomes identical with the honor of God.

Becket is a more complex character than Antigone and Joan who play their roles with youthful fervor, feeling intuitively that somewhere, somehow they are right in doing what they do. More logical, Becket controls his feelings and does not permit himself the moments of weakness which make Joan and Antigone temporarily waver in their causes. Antigone and Joan, who die young, are spared the debasing effects of life, and, for them, as for the sixteen-year-old monk who dies in the cathedral at Becket's side, "this black world will have been in order to the end" (262). To Antigone, the bitter truth about Polynices comes as a revelation, just as Joan is stunned to learn that her best friends have forsaken her. Having lived longer, Becket knows about the Polyniceses of this world. In him, Antigone's determination to fight for an ideal is combined with Creon's rich experience of life.

Like the ending of *L'Alouette,* the ending of *Becket* barely conceals bitter irony. The king, who has had Becket murdered, entrusts the inquiry into his murder to none other than one of Becket's assassins, and, moreover, forced to act in just that way for reasons of political expediency, he hastens to acknowledge publicly his total solidarity with his dead friend's views, vying before the Saxon crowd for a share in Becket's posthumous glory.

Becket, a "rebel at forty," represents Anouilh's last attempt to depict metaphysical rebellion in all its vainglorious splendor.

Antigone, Joan and Becket belong to the period of history prior to 1789 to which Camus in *L'Homme révolté* refers as the age of negation. In the history of rebellion, the age of negation is an age in which the rebel contents himself with bare pronouncement. This is the age of metaphysical rebellion, an often suicidal type of rebellion in the course of

which an assertion is made and upheld for no other apparent
reason than that of its own beauty, leaving behind perhaps no
more than bewilderment and surprise on the part of those
unable to comprehend acts that are seemingly gratuitous and
futile. Metaphysical rebellion appears more concerned with
the essence of truth than its ethical angle, and the rebels who
espouse it firmly believe that there are essences which must
be served and from time to time enriched by exemplary
sacrifices.

The historical event which, according to Camus, consecrates the end of the age of negation and leads into the age of
ideologies is the decapitation of Louis XVI in 1793, a regi-
cide which was at the same time a deicide. The by-now classic
sentence, which better than any other speaks for the sudden
change in the quality of rebellion, is the warning given Louis
XVI: "No, sire, this is not a rebellion, it is a revolution."

Elaborating upon the differences between rebellion and
revolution, Camus, after questioning whether revolution characterizes or betrays the value of rebellion, comes to view
revolution as the logical outcome of metaphysical rebellion.
Revolution is an historical rebellion, a movement originating
in the realm of ideas and consisting of the injection of ideas
into historical experience, fostered by the use of brute force.

The historical personage leading the way into the age of
ideologies, whom Anouilh has made into the hero of *Pauvre
Bitos ou Le Dîner de têtes,* is Robespierre.

## 5. HISTORICAL REBELLION: *PAUVRE BITOS*

*Pauvre Bitos ou Le Dîner de têtes,* is one of Anouilh's most Pirandellian plays. One of the characters in the play, Maxime, acts as the stage manager. Much like the Director in Pirandello's *Sei personaggi in cerca d'autore,* he comments upon the action and initiates the spectator to the secrets of stagecraft by demonstrating how persons become personages and theatrical acting, a poetic dream. Maxime stages an unusual game. He has invited a group of friends to a "dinner of heads" requesting that they dress their heads so as to achieve the greatest possible resemblance to certain figures of 1789 and, at the same time, that they refresh their memories with some pertinent historical data. They must be well prepared to receive the guest of honor, André Bitos, the local deputy public prosecutor whom Maxime hates, and whom the guests in general dislike, because of his Jacobinistic attitude in

47

matters of justice. In the early 1950's, at the time when
Maxime and his wealthy friends are reveling in an atmosphere
of political, economic and social *live and let live,* savoring the
"sweet life" in a provincial town near Paris, André Bitos is
prosecuting delinquents, criminals and, most particularly, former Nazi collaborators with an intransigency and zeal that
have earned him the nickname of "The Incorruptible." No
wonder then that Maxime has asked Bitos to come to his
dinner in the guise of Robespierre. The purpose of the wig
party is thus revealed. Posing as Danton, Mirabeau, Saint-
Just, Tallien and some other notables of 1789, Maxime and
his group of liberals, composed of country squires and capi-
talists, intend to convey to the disguised Bitos what in other
circumstances they would never dare tell him face to face for
fear of his judicial authority. According to Maxime's plan,
Bitos, the target of the evening, must be exposed to merciless
attack. His conservative political views, his proletarian sensi-
tivities, his social ambitions, and his moral physiognomy
must be laid bare and ridiculed until André Bitos' entire
personality is torn to shreds and there remains nothing of
him but a moral carcass disclosed in all its lamentable naked-
ness.

When Bitos-Robespierre arrives, the dinner begins. What
starts as an elegant and amusing game soon degenerates into a
spiteful, venomous debate in the course of which neither side
is spared. Due to Maxime's determination to annihilate Bitos
completely, by the time the main course is served the game
has already far exceeded the limits of fair play, and Bitos
feels trapped. During the first act, Anouilh gradually creates
on stage an atmosphere in which reality and illusion, the
actors and their masks, become so fused that the spectator
can hardly discern the play from the more and more promi-

nently emerging play within the play. At moments, the spectator is so caught up in the game that he is willing to believe that the action on stage is taking place in 1789. But the mirage gives way from time to time and a sense of contemporaneity is re-established whenever an actor steps out of his role, briefly removing his wig for instance. In a matter of seconds, Anouilh swings the play back and forth between the periods of the First and the Fourth Republics until the dinner's climactic moment, when, just in time for dessert, the last unexpected guest makes his entrance: a young, recently released delinquent whom Bitos sent to jail many years earlier. The late arrival comes disguised as Constable Merda, the man who, on the day in 1794 which marked the end of the Reign of Terror, forced his way through the crowd gathered in the City Hall and fired a shot at Robespierre, wounding him in the jaw. All the dinner guests, except the stage manager Maxime, who planned this last-minute surprise, are seized with uneasy premonitions about what will happen, with which the play within the play gains additional credibility. At the sight of the young man, the panic-stricken Bitos mechanically continues playing the role of Robespierre as if in a dream; while "Merda," who slowly draws nearer to him, speaks as if he were reciting from Michelet or Taine:

> The Young Man: ... And the policeman Merda forced his way through the crowd which had gathered in the Town Hall Assembly Room. He went straight to Robespierre. 'Are you Citizen Robespierre? I arrest you.'

> Bitos: (as in a dream) You are a traitor! It is *I* who'll have *you* arrested.

> The Young Man: (with an intimation of a smile on his
> face) . . . said Robespierre . . . But the policeman
> Merda, who was not at all in the style of the period
> (in that he was not skilled in oratory), concluded
> that there was no point in talking any further. So
> he took out his gun . . . (425-26)

whereupon the young man brandishes a small period piece
gun and fires. The lights go out in the midst of general
confusion, with Bitos clutching his jaw. When they come
back on again, the actors and their masks have completely
fused. The spectator is invited to witness what took place on
the day of Robespierre's execution in *l'an II de l'Egalité*,
embarking on a journey back into the Reign of Terror.

In Act Two, Bitos-Robespierre, who is lying in a faint, is
dreaming. The spectator witnesses his dream, presented on
stage in tableaux showing: (1) Robespierre as a little boy
attending the Jesuit fathers' preparatory school, being
flogged by the headmaster for being overly proud; (2) Robespierre as a young deputy from the district of Arras, being
shown the door by the marquis de Mirabeau after a heated
political discussion in which Robespierre exalts the nascent
revolution destined to sweep away the insouciant, self-
satisfied parasites of the *Ancien Régime;* (3) Robespierre in
power, discussing with his alter ego, Saint-Just, the necessity
of political purges in the interest of the good of the people;
(4) Robespierre dining in Tallien's country home with his
friends Danton and Camille Desmoulins at a time when he is
already determined to have both Danton and Desmoulins
liquidated on account of their deviations from the true revolutionary path and their lapses into bourgeois comfort; (5)
Robespierre dictating to Saint-Just his famous *Loi de prairial,*
consecrating murder in the interest of the good of the people.

As Bitos recovers from his fainting spell, his dreams fade away, and during most of Act Three we see Maxime and his friends doing their best to persuade an outraged Bitos that the wig party was but an innocent little game.

The structure of *Pauvre Bitos* follows a simple pattern. In Act One, the game being staged by Maxime slowly imposes itself upon the reality of the play and progresses toward a climax. In Act Two, the heart of the play, the game completely submerges the reality of the play. Act Three brings release from tension, as reality gradually re-establishes its prerogatives, and the characters, who have been identified for a moment with historical personages, conform once more to the standards of daily life in a small provincial town.

Anouilh uses the character of the compromiser André Bitos as a vehicle by which to introduce the heroic character of Robespierre on stage. The blending of their two personalities and of the times they live in, gives Anouilh the opportunity to comment on more than a hundred and fifty years of French history, and to make a ferocious attack against the age of ideologies with its many institutions for the promotion of legal murder and terror, advocated in the name of the supposed will of the majority. In *L'Alouette* a devastating judgment is already aimed at the period of modern history, inaugurated by the French Revolution, the period of the rise to power of the underdog, the "poor and virtuous" son of the people who comes to supplant the libertines of noble birth who triumphed in the days of the *Ancien Régime*. The words are put into the mouth of Charles VII and are delivered like a prophecy:

> Everything will be attempted. Men of lower class origin will become masters of kingdoms, for several centuries— the time of the passage of a meteor in the sky—and this

then will be the period of massacres and most monstrous errors.

Charles speaks of the coming of cynical men who, in
future centuries, will rise to power through sheer villainy,
misleading the people with abstract ideas about the organiza-
tion of happiness. Filled with highsounding words about
absolute freedom, these men, so very concerned with the
welfare of their fellow citizens, will bring about the worst
enslavement of the masses known to history.

> And on the day of judgment, when it comes to adding
> up the figures, it will be seen that the most debauched
> and the most capricious of kings did less harm to the
> world than one of those virtuous men. (61)

Robespierre is the first in a long line of modern saints
who kill people "for their own good."

In *Pauvre Bitos,* with sparkling, satirical wit, Anouilh
directs barbs at both the political left and right, ridicules the
traditional French institutions—the judiciary, the parliament
and the armed forces—offers a brilliant lesson in philosophy,
history and sociology, exposes the sham of the political
kitchens of the First and Fourth Republics and puts across
some of the most grating lines he ever wrote without their
interfering with either the dynamic stage action or the plausi-
bility of the characters. Anouilh masterfully uses and trans-
forms the Pirandellian mold, but in addition to the theatrical
bravura he achieves with the play-within-the-play technique
and the particular variant he gives to the duality of personality theme, he introduces a new perspective to his play. The
wealth of historical, political and philosophical material he

integrates into *Pauvre Bitos* points to a consciousness enriched by the lessons of World War Two and the post-war years. Anouilh shows French history since 1789 to be nothing more than a stage for the practice of legal murder with *heads* featured as the national dish. This explains the meaning of the play's subtitle *The Dinner of Heads.* It is, to be sure, a wig party for which the guests are supposed to dress their heads, but at the same time Anouilh invites everybody to witness a spectacular washing of blood-drenched and mud-soiled linen accumulated in the course of two centuries of French history.

Hardly anyone playing a role in politics emerges unscathed from Anouilh's "surprise party." The rightwingers are found guilty of inexcusable laxity and addiction to facility and carelessness—from those aristocrats in 1792 who instead of mounting barricades and defending themselves against their exterminators, meekly accepted the verdict of the guillotine, retaining to the very end their ridiculous habit of generous tipping—down to those modern upper-class ladies whose leanings toward modern varieties of Jacobinism, notably drawing-room communism are classified as peculiar side-effects of the menopause. Political leftism, be it socialism, communism or certain types of democracy, is alluded to as a vast money-making enterprise under the pretext of taking care of the people. But by far the most despicable products of humanity on Anouilh's political stage seem to be the political opportunists, collaborationists and turncoats, the *bastillards,* as they are called in *Pauvre Bitos* and in *L'Hurluberlu,* or "excrements in silk stockings," as they are referred to in *La Foire d'Empoigne.*

The term *bastillard,* is used to denote the large number of individuals who, in the days of the First Republic, were in

possession of false certificates testifying to the effect that on
July 14, 1789, they had been present on the Place de la
Bastille, active participants in the storming of the prison.
Such certificates were ultimate proofs of good citizenship
and gave their bearers political security, as well as the likeli-
hood of securing better positions. By way of analogy, the
term as used by Anouilh refers to the individuals who, in
1944 and 1945, right after the liberation of France in the
course of World War Two, were given high positions for
having participated in the French Resistance against the Germans, or, like their "ancestors" of 1789, for having false
certificates stating that in one way or another they had
contributed to the fight against Fascism, when in fact some
of these certificate bearers were probably collaborationists.

Since so many political exponents and practitioners
found themselves under attack on Anouilh's stage, it can
readily be understood why the first performances of the play
turned into a real *bataille du Pauvre Bitos*. The *Tout Paris*
audience of the gala opening booed the play. The press
reflected the mood of the first-night public in its nearly
unanimous condemnation of the play and the author. The
rightist *Le Figaro* and *L'Aurore* agreed with the leftist *L'Hu-
manité* that Anouilh had written an outrageous play un-
worthy of his talent. However, when performed before the
*grand public, Pauvre Bitos* received ovations.

Political passions aroused by the early performances of
*Pauvre Bitos* in 1956 were further inflamed by the "recent
events" in Hungary. In October, November and December
1956, violent reactions could be expected in the Théâtre
Montparnasse-Gaston Baty, right after the following ex-
change of lines between Robespierre, dictating the notorious
Prairial Laws, and Saint-Just:

> Robespierre: Paragraph five: To defend traitors means to conspire. The law provides as defenders for calumnied patriots patriotic members of the jury. It does not provide such for conspirators!
>
> Saint-Just: Retroactivity. Prejudiced jurors. No defense. It's a model of its kind. It will serve again . . . (470)

At this point, shouts of "Budapest . . . Budapest . . . " rose from a number of audiences in 1956, impressed by the similarity between the Reign of Terror in France in 1794 and the Reign of Terror in Hungary after the suppression of the Budapest rebellion by Russian troops. Hundreds of Hungarian patriots had been accused of treason and sentenced to death "in the interest of the good of the people" in expedient, hastily staged trials. For a short while, these events gave special meaning to certain passages in *Pauvre Bitos,* which the spectators of 1956 were quick to grasp.

It was necessary for political passions to subside before a more objective evaluation of Anouilh's masterpiece could be afforded. Placed in its proper perspective within the larger whole of Anouilh's dramatic output, *Pauvre Bitos* appears in a completely different light; a character play above anything else. From the *Grand Guignol* of history, Anouilh chose here the impassive mask of Robespierre in order to animate it on stage. He endowed the superficially inhuman and almost monstrous textbook portrait of Robespierre with profound humanity. Deep inside the character of Robespierre, Anouilh discovered the voice of a child who had been hurt, the voice of an outraged innocence which had been deformed in its contact with the world. Anouilh parallels the youthful disappointments suffered by Bitos and Robespierre and presents the adult life of his twin-heroes as a carefully planned and minutely elaborated revenge against all of mankind for the humiliations experienced at the hand of others during their youth. In the moral of his fable *Le Loup et la vipère,* which sheds light upon his treatment of Robespierre's character, Anouilh muses about the many thousands of people who would have died at home in bed instead of under the guillotine or in gas chambers, had Robespierre's and Hitler's childhoods perchance been happy.[1] The inhumanity of other men caused Robespierre to harden, to exterminate his heart, that weak spot of the intellect. The real criminal then is not Robespierre, but the other people who wronged him and, implicitly, all of nature for having produced such people.

Nature is described as inhuman:

> Nature too decimates, sweeps away, cleanses, kills off. Every single day nature brings to life and exterminates millions of beings. A day in the world is but a huge cycle of successive births and annihilations so that nature's plan can be accomplished. (412)

In promoting murder as a means of revenge for the humiliations suffered in his youth, Robespierre cynically identifies himself with nature. By killing, like Camus' Caligula, he pretends to compete with God. The Cult of the Supreme Being he inaugurates represents the substitution of a human god for the metaphysical God served by rebels like Antigone and Joan of Arc. Robespierre's rebellion is nihilistic, characterized by the famous statement: "Everything is just," signifying at the same time that in fact nothing is just and that everything is possible.

A conqueror, defiantly alone on the stage, repeatedly

compelled to brush some imaginary fleck of dust from his jacket in order to be perfectly clean and pure, Robespierre incarnates historical rebellion carried to its extreme of absolute negation. He embodies a desperate search for a sort of microcosmic unity within an absurd macrocosm, showing at what cost of exacting self-discipline, exaltation of will and disregard for means, the ideal of purity can be preserved beyond childhood and youth. It is, no doubt, a perverted, murderous ideal of purity, yet, as we are subtly led to believe, there is nothing wrong with the ideal itself. Robespierre's ideal suffered degradation in contact with life, to the point of justifying murder for the sake of its survival. In the final analysis, the character of Robespierre offers a devastating insight into what time does to an ideal—to what happens to rebellion at "forty."

In the *Pièces brillantes,* in contrast to the *Pièces roses,* Anouilh shows what happens to love once the innocence and the charm of youth are gone. At thirty-seven and thirty-eight, Héro and Tigre in *La Répétition* still speak the same words and make the same gestures as Anouilh's lovers in the dawn of their lives. They lack the fervor of youth; their hearts are no longer in harmony with their words, but they are not yet grotesque. A few not too bleak years lie ahead before they become like General Saint-Pé in *La Valse des toréadors.*

The same could be said of rebellion in relation to the age of the rebel. Like love at "forty," rebellion at "forty" is still possible, although it lacks the enthusiasm and the spontaneity of youth. It is not yet grotesque, as it becomes in *L'Hurluberlu ou Le Réactionnaire amoureux.*

> Wanting to be a hero is not enough. Neither
> courage nor the gift suffices. There must be
> hydras and dragons. There were none in sight.
>
> (Sartre, *Les Mots*)

## 6. REBELLION WITHOUT A CAUSE:
### *L'HURLUBERLU* AND *LA FOIRE D'EMPOIGNE*

Ludovic, the *hurluberlu*, the "fighting cock," the hero of
*L'Hurluberlu ou Le Réactionnaire amoureux*, is a fifty-two-
year-old retired general, who lives in his country home with
his wife, sister and children during the late 1950's. In 1940,
Ludovic was among the first to join the Resistance movement
against Marshal Pétain and the Germans. He did so on the
spur of the moment, attracted by what then struck him as a
perfectly desperate cause. However, the desperate cause triumphed in the end, and by August 23, 1944, the day of the
Liberation of Paris, Ludovic was a reluctant hero of the
French Resistance. He could have accepted the honors and
rewards that come with victory, yet, his duty accomplished,
he preferred to retire from the world. He did not consider the
mere luck of being on the winning side a sufficient reason to
be honored, just as he felt uncomfortable seeing his former
colleagues who had served under Pétain being dishonored,

58

simply because they had not had the luck to end up among the victors.

Ludovic's modesty and gentlemanliness proved somewhat exceptional at a time when many who had not resisted at all were boasting about their participation in the Resistance, producing questionable proofs of their self-asserted involvement in the common cause. In 1945 Ludovic was the first to spot the rise to power of these *bastillards*—with a clear-sightedness that prompted him to stage a new rebellion, this time against the very "liberators" of France. The plot failed, and Ludovic wound up in prison. Released six months later, he found himself sacked. He then married a woman half his age with whom he moved to the country, determined to write his war memoirs.

> I write the title at the top of the page: Chapter One. For a moment I lay my pen on the table in order to think . . . and I realize that I have absolutely nothing to say. (12)

This bitter revelation could have been fatal for the General had not an important discovery followed in its wake. Ludovic suddenly became aware of the presence in France of a most dangerous enemy, *the maggots* as he calls them, alluding to the members of the mediocre race and the race of compromisers who have penetrated into the national organism by posing as friends of the people, heroes of the Resistance, dispensers of social welfare and advocates of democratic principles.

According to the General, the maggots are totally devoid of patriotic feeling. The fruit interests them only as a place into which to burrow.

As a true patriot and untiring fighter, Ludovic plans a
new rebellion. At the beginning of the play, we discover that
he has founded an anti-vermin conspiracy, a group including
an impoverished baron, an aging playboy, the family doctor
and the local ironmonger. As the play develops, the General
utters a number of urgent warnings against the danger of the
vermin spreading in today's world and in France in particular.
According to him, the vermin are multiplying everywhere.
Government, business and the arts are infested with worms
who, hidden in the safety of their holes, dictate the tone of
modern life. As a result of this infestation, more and more
people tend to sit on upholstery that is made softer every
year to suit the growing trend toward comfort without effort, money without sweat, ideas without thinking, taste
without the bother of acquiring it and sports without the
bother of going to the stadium. In business, the concern for
quality and solidity of merchandise has been sacrificed to the
exclusive goal of the fast turnover. The theatre has become
flooded with gloomy anti-plays disseminating vermin under
the label of metaphysical anguish.

While thundering against the many evils of modern times,
the General is reminded by the more rational characters in the
play of the pervading historical trend toward democracy and
liberalism, of the great modern economic and demographic
facts, of the inalienable rights of the masses, of the changing
morals of the younger generation, all powerful components
of an irrefutable reality. But for Ludovic there is no irrefutable reality, no trend of history, no rights of the masses. The
General scoffs at the economists and their supposedly important facts and findings. He denies any special prerogatives for
the greatest number. To him, a thousand imbeciles are nothing but one imbecile multiplied by a thousand, and he does

not understand why anyone should be more concerned about a thousand of them than about one. Like Antigone, Ludovic rejects *a priori* any attempt at trying to understand arguments in favor of moderation and compromise. Like Robespierre in *Pauvre Bitos,* he condemns facility and pleads for the highest professional excellence. Like Molière's Alceste, he prefers to lose a friend rather than to suppress a truth. And, like Rostand's Cyrano he voices a contemptible *no* to the values upheld by the mediocre race and an enthusiastic *yes* to the values dear to his heart.

Ludovic's conservative philosophy is rooted in the concept of the essential man. In the General's opinion, whatever the developments that history, politics, economics and science may hold in store, the essential man will always remain what he has been: handsome or ugly, intelligent or stupid, endowed with or devoid of a sense of honor. Ludovic opposes eternal human nature to the concept of the socially-rooted man who, according to a train of thought from the naturalists to the existentialists, cannot escape his *situation.* The General is not interested in the human situation, only in man as such. Therefore, in the reformed tomorrow he envisages, it is the humanists who will have precedence over the economists. In keeping with his basic philosophy, the General's practical program is geared toward giving the highest possible example of leadership, at reinstating a taste for strictness, austerity, hard work and, possibly, in some cases, even at provoking a nostalgia for honor. As to the means by which to bring to power an ideal government devoted to the propagation of an aristocratic code of behavior, Ludovic limits himself to saying that the future belongs to active minorities. Reminded that a real application of his ultra-conservative philosophy would set back the clock of history a

good two hundred years, Ludovic imperturbably retorts:
"Why not, if for the past two centuries we have been travel-
ling along on the wrong track" (74). In his denunciation of
modern technocratic civilization, Ludovic goes so far as to
question whether man has not in fact retrograded by aban-
doning imagination and poetry as instruments of scientific
investigation. Upholding these and similar views, Ludovic is
bound to face one disappointment and defeat after another.

He learns that his top-secret conspiracy has been common
knowledge for quite some time and is, in fact, the laughing
stock of the entire town. To counteract the breach of secrecy
that has been committed, the General is prepared to reform
his group and work for a while in deep illegality, but at this
point, his friends refuse to follow him. The doctor, concerned about his clientele, backs out for fear of public
scandal. The aging playboy suddenly discovers himself to be a
democrat who previously was unaware of his true inclina-
tions. And Baron Bélazor, Ludovic's surest friend, quits because he must make a good impression on the town council-
lor Michepain to whom he is indebted for a sizeable loan for
the restoration of his crumbling castle. Ludovic even has
trouble in his own household where he must face his daughter's desertion and listen to his wife's lectures concerning the
futility and absurdity of his rebellion.

But the General pays no attention to any of these admoni-
tions. Betrayed and alone, he continues to fight, in an infested country where, according to him, a few Communists,
abstract painters, royal highnesses and bicycle-racers figure as
the most envied and talked about social elite, where top-rank-
ing industrialists amuse themselves by voting as far to the left
as their workmen, where funds that regulate the life of the
nation are dispensed or withheld at will by small-time dema-
gogues like Michepain and where vulgar and primitive individ-

uals, like Ludovic's neighbor, the Milkman, play important roles in small community councils. These people have no understanding whatsoever of the General's aristocratic code of behavior, and when he challenges them to a duel with a classic slap in the face they respond with a contemporary punch in the jaw The General must touch the ground twice, first, knocked down by his daughter's suitor, the son of a manufacturer of plastic goods, next, beaten up by the Milkman, under the very eyes of his eight-year-old son Toto, who believes that his father can do whatever he promises to do. Toto and Ledadu, the simple-minded local ironmonger who speaks with reverence of the good old days of the wooden spoon, remain the General's only disciples and faithful followers in the end. In the course of meaningful conversations with Toto, the General formulates his philosophy of life, which is in fact no more than an abridged version of Joan's "lesson in courage" to Charles in *L'Alouette*. He teaches Toto that in a battle, when afraid, instead of running backwards, one should run forwards and that so long as one isn't dead, there is always a chance for recovery. In the final scene of *L'Hurluberlu*, in which we see father and son munching *mininistafia*,[1] to help them both overcome a momentary depression, the General goes so far as to compare himself to Joan of Arc. He promises Toto that despite the Milkman's apparent greater physical strength, he will take care of things and pay the arrogant neighbor a visit to teach the villain a lesson in knightship and honor. As Toto cannot master his concern for his father on account of the Milkman's impressive athletic frame, the General asks:

General: Do you know the story of Joan of Arc and the English?

Toto: Yes.

General: She wasn't the stronger one either.

Toto:    Alright, but you are not Joan of Arc!

General: (Thunderstruck) True. (Adding after a while)
         But you forget, Toto, that in the beginning,
         she wasn't Joan of Arc either.

Toto:    Who was she then?

General: A helpless little shepherdess. Given the circum-
         stances, there was nothing she could do, noth-
         ing at all. And yet you see what came out of it!

Toto:    (With unperturbed logic) All right, but there was
         God!

General: (Gently, after a while) But we must hope that
         God is still around, Toto . . . (157-58)

Toto is willing to believe his father. But the others find
the General ridiculous, particularly the local authorities who,
although they know about Ludovic's plans, do nothing to
stop his conspiracy against the world and mankind. "Don't
worry, they won't even bother putting you in jail" (135), the
general is told by his daughter's suitor, who incarnates the
wisdom of a twentieth-century Creon. Paradoxically, in
*L'Hurluberlu,* Creon's and Antigone's roles are reversed, as
reason speaks through the mouth of a twenty-year-old, while
undaunted passion finds its mouthpiece in a man in his
fifties.[2] But, hard as he tries, Ludovic lacks the power to stir
other people. Like General Saint-Pé in *La Valse des toréadors,* he has the bad luck to have the heart of a boy
pounding in the carcass of an old man. Besides, times have
considerably changed since the days of Joan of Arc. In 1959,
the year of Ludovic's conspiracy against the maggots, there
no longer seem to be any great causes with which the heroes
can identify. Ludovic's quixotic rebellion represents a desperate attempt on the part of the hero to discover such a cause
at any price.

In *La Foire d'Empoigne,* Anouilh goes even farther in showing how, in the age of ideologies, there is no place left for rebellions like Antigone's and Joan's. In this play the stage is completely dominated by the compromisers while the role of the hero is one of secondary importance. Twenty-two-year-old Lieutenant d'Anouville, the only survivor of one of Napoleon's light infantry regiments, seeks a cause which would give meaning to his life. He tells his idol, Napoleon, who is on the verge of deportation to Saint-Helena, of his readiness to sacrifice his life for him. But Napoleon, very much annoyed by such an untimely display of heroism, refuses the offer.

> No, absolutely not. First of all, you have plenty of time. And then, with you, nobody would be interested. There has been no shortage of deaths lately, you know.

In Napoleon's opinion, since the French Revolution and since Waterloo in particular, the times have become unpropitious for heroes. It is as if all the great roles were played out by 1815. At the end of *La Foire d'Empoigne,* Napoleon tries to decide what d'Anouville's chances may be if the boy absolutely insists on choosing the heroic path. "Cover yourself with glory, if that still can be done," he tells the foolhardy would-be hero, advising:

> Why not shoot fat Louis or become a carbonaro? I am sure there is still some future in Jacobinism. In France they haven't squeezed that lemon dry yet. Good luck! If my mail is forwarded, you can write me all about your plans. (279)

Napoleon's ironic departure from the stage of history and his final message to d'Anouville bear further witness to the

decline of rebellion in the modern age as they bring down the
curtain not only on *La Foire d'Empoigne* but on Anouilh's
illustrations of rebellion for a cause.

If Anouilh's message concerning the historical evolution
of rebellion is a dark one, his attitude toward the spirit of
rebellion is highly optimistic. In spite of the adversity of
history and the silence of God, Anouilh's "fighting cocks"
are compelled to go on fighting forever. Anouilh consecrates
in them the greatness of the man of courage who, abandoned
by all and prostrate on the ground, continues to get up to
fight for his cause as long as he lives.

Life is chipping away at me . . . It is working on
a masterpiece . . . I must help it . . . I must let it
complete its work.

(Cocteau, *Orphée*)


## 7. REBELLION OF THE ARTIST

In 1968, after six years without a new Anouilh play
performed in Paris, Anouilh returned to the stage with *Le
Boulanger, la Boulangère et le Petit Mitron,* followed by *Cher
Antoine ou l'Amour raté* in 1969, *Les Poissons rouges ou
"Mon Père ce héros"* and *Ne réveillez pas Madame* in 1970
and *Tu étais si gentil quand tu étais petit* and *Le Directeur de
l'Opéra* in 1972. The *noir* is blacker now, the *grinçant* more
jarring and the *brillant* more sparkling. Earlier variations of
Anouilh's absurd hero were the rebel against time, the rebel
against environment, the rebel for a cause, the conqueror.
Now Anouilh focuses on the most exalted of all rebels, the
artist. He speaks through his Playwrights of his one lasting
love—the theatre. For a last celebration before the final
curtain, Anouilh "invites into the castle" all the stock characters from his previous plays. The twenty-year-old girls reappear but the aging heroes[1] no longer trust them having
learned that it is in the nature of twenty-year-old girls to
betray promises and abandon love for the security of marriage. The young girls inevitably, almost overnight, begin
resembling their mothers, become nagging wives addicted to
comfort and luxury before turning into *les générales* and,

67

ultimately, into healthy widows who pay regular visits to
their husbands' graves. The hour of divorces, deaths and
widowhoods has struck on Anouilh's stage. The only marriage celebrated in this late period of the *noir* and the
*grinçant* is that of a fifteen-year-old pregnant daughter.[2] The
children pay for the mistakes of their parents while waiting
their turn to make the same mistakes. The world they live in
leaves little place for the healthy development of individual-
ity. The text of *Les Poissons rouges* develops further the
commentary on the sad state of the world's affairs voiced in
*L'Hurluberlu* ten years earlier. Now in place of referring to a
*maggot-infested* society Anouilh refers to a world dominated
by *hunchbacks*. To stand erect, firmly planted on one's two
feet, chin up and spine straight, expressing openly one's
thoughts is considered a major sin bound to be punished
sooner or later. In an era of triumphant conformity, egalitari-
anism and mass production the individual is better off bent.
The earlier he develops a hump the more integrated a member of society he will be.[3] Anouilh makes his Playwrights
repeat his flamboyant belief in individual freedom. Man is
free to relieve himself on *les poissons rouges* if he so chooses.
The Playwright did so as a child in an aquarium and continues to do so on stage as an adult man. It is an unpopular
approach in today's world which caters to the *poissons
rouges* but freedom means most of all the freedom to act
against fashionable trends. With even greater brio than before
Anouilh links the action on stage to certain historical arche-
types. The father, the mother and the son in *Le Boulanger, la
Boulangère et le Petit Mitron* are also Louis XVI, Marie-
Antoinette and the Dauphin, the prototype of a disunited
family brought together for the first time through suffering,
on the eve of execution. Toto who loves to read history

books is the "family's dauphin" who dreams of a last minute family apotheosis. In *Les Poissons rouges* the Playwright relives various periods of his family life as a part of the life of a larger family—France: amorous betrayals at home are paralleled with political betrayals in the nation. In *Cher Antoine* Anouilh imagines through the Playwright his "own death in the castle" likening the ending of his own play to the ending of Chekhov's *The Cherry Orchard* where, after all the doors have been locked, it turns out that an old servant has been left behind in the abandoned family home. The old servant is Anouilh himself, the eternal prisoner of the theatre where alone, after everyone has left, he remains imagining new situations into which to place his characters who need new texts to make themselves heard. At the end of *Ne réveillez pas Madame,* the Playwright remains alone on stage, old, exhausted, exasperated. At the end of yet another rehearsal, he comments on the impasse of success and the difficulty of continuing when so close to the end of the road. In anticipating his own end, Anouilh experiences the agonies of old age through his playwrights and directors, constantly reevaluating the changing world around him, continuing to write the moral history of our century in the light of his own spiritual odyssey. His repeated efforts bring to mind the passage from *Le Mythe de Sisyphe* in which Camus writes about the most distinguishing mark of the great artist:

> A man's sole creation is strengthened in its successive and multiple aspects: his works. One after another, they complement one another, correct or overtake one another, contradict one another too. If something brings creation to an end, it is not the victorious and illusory cry of the blinded artist: "I have said everything," but

the death of the creator which closes his experience and the book of his genius.[4]

Antoine, the hero of *Cher Antoine,* and Antoine, the hero of *Les Poissons rouges,* are playwrights. Julien, the hero of *Ne réveillez pas Madame,* a total man of the theatre like Molière, is a stage director, theatre manager, actor and playwright. Antonio, the hero of *Le Directeur de l'Opéra* is the manager of "the world in a microcosm," the opera house. He is a contemporary Atlas tricked by life into "shouldering a planet," a reluctant Christ "placed under a cross," a victim of the consumer society, obliged to write checks left and right to help keep the outfit afloat. His bored, aging, wasteful wife and his gluttonous mother-in-law are forever reproachful, his daughters and his son-in-law are burdensome with their insatiable appetites and many weaknesses, but worst of all, his son Toto, the only bright spot in the lives of Anouilh's earlier *hurluberlus* has grown up. Toto is no longer eight as he was in *L'Hurluberlu, Le Boulanger, la Boulangère et le Petit Mitron* and *Les Poissons rouges* but twenty and like the other members of the family brutally selfish, critical of his father and in need of money to pay off his gambling debts and his mistresses. As if his family problems were not enough, Antonio must put up with a strike by organized labor in the theatre, in a world where those who have nothing and consequently need not fear to lose anything represent a perpetual threat.

Time has also taken its toll as is most clearly symbolized on the stage by the cleaning woman *la grosse Jeanne,* a monstrous old hag who a few decades earlier had given Antonio his greatest sensual pleasure. The sound of a vacuum cleaner as it is pushed by *la grosse Jeanne* is heard throughout the last scene of *Le Directeur de l'Opéra,* a reminder that the time of life has come for the hero when it is necessary for him to clean up his house and leave. Even though after excessive use, his feelings are considerably dulled, Antonio is ready to fall in love with Toto's abandoned mistress and assume the paternity of Toto's discarded son, a potential new Toto in his life. Gently rejected and reminded of his actual station on the road of life Antonio recovers just in time to attend the rehearsal of an opera, a typical eighteenth century musical piece very much like Rossini's *The Barber of Seville,* in which the characters who play important parts in Antonio's life appear appropriately costumed to remind Antonio in song that there is a time to love and a time to have loved and that once love is gone the last mistress, Death, waits to receive the incurable lover in his last bed.

Antonio's rebellion at this very late moment in life consists in the mere fact of his continuing to function in spite of all the unfavorable circumstances. The time has come in the life of Anouilh's heroes when, after having exhausted every other kind of rebellion, the act alone of continuing to breathe represents a kind of rebellion. After all the blows he had suffered, Antonio could have chosen to end his life in the style of commander di Santi-Pellegrini, firing a shot through his monocle. Instead he chose to go on, to don once more his director's costume, and, as he had done all his life, to appear where scheduled in the performance of his duty.

Earlier types of rebellion in Anouilh's theatre provoked their own particular endings. The deaths of heroes like Antigone, Joan, Becket and Robespierre were so many variations on a similar type of exit from the stage of life. The death of the artist calls for altogether different final scenes. The death of Molière shortly after a seizure suffered on stage while as Argan pretending to be seriously ill could hardly be improved on. In the case of a legendary artist in another domaine, Don Juan, Anouilh improved on this hero's ending by having the aging seducer Ornifle in *Ornifle ou Le Courant d'air,* die of a stroke while on his way to yet another of his rendez-vous. For an artist there can be no better timed ending, real or imaginary, than being felled by the "commander" while involved in his most passionate activity. One can only hope that Anouilh's last outing be as successful, that his "last mistress" come upon him during a rehearsal on a day when he will have the manuscript of a newly completed play in his breast pocket. On stage or in life, it will no longer matter, for Anouilh has made a specialty of blending the two into one, of redeeming life through illusion and illusion through life. "To create means to live twice" writes Camus in *L'Homme révolté.* It also means to die twice: the first time for Anouilh symbolically on stage as in *Cher Antoine* or slowly agonizing in *Ne réveillez pas Madame* and *Le Directeur de l'Opéra,* as his doppelgängers discover the last truths.

Viewed from the perspective of the early seventies, we may still expect from Anouilh a number of new plays that "he will be unable to write,"[5] in which he will pronounce new funeral orations over his dead body and take more farewell bows after which his second death may seem almost no more than another of his stage effects—the longest silence after the longest of his plays.

> The honor of man, Toto, you must preserve it.
> It is your heritage . . . It is after all you who
> invented Electricity, built the Chartres cathe-
> dral, wrote Pascal's *Pensées* . . . And Molière's
> plays, all of them they are yours too! And the
> plays of Shakespeare! You must never forget
> this, Toto!
>
> (Anouilh, *Les Poissons rouges*)

## 8. CONCLUSION

Anouilh's dramatic opus reflects an imposing scope of vision and diversity of tone. Anouilh has the comical verve of Molière and the elegance of Marivaux, the skill and light touch of a boulevard entertainer and the intellectual power of a popular philosopher. Critics have compared him to Sardou, Guitry, Labiche, Salacrou, Giraudoux and Shakespeare. Anouilh himself has named the authors to whom he feels most indebted. He speaks of his deep reverence for Molière. Rimbaud is his preferred poet. Then come Feydeau, Rostand, Bataille, Giraudoux, Claudel and Pirandello. Each of these authors has contributed something to Anouilh's outlook on the world. Through his modern versions of ancient myths in *Antigone, Eurydice, Médée* and *Tu étais si gentil quand tu étais petit,* Anouilh is an heir to Aeschylus, Euripides and Sophocles. For both his intellectual content and his expression, Anouilh is an heir to the moralist tradition in French literature, an heir to Montaigne, Pascal, La Rochefoucauld, La Bruyère, Vauvenargues and Chamfort.

*Antigone, L'Alouette, Becket, Pauvre Bitos, L'Hurlu-berlu, La Foire d'Empoigne* and *Les Poissons rouges* best

73

represent a moral, political and, to a certain extent, philosophical theatre in Anouilh's opus. However, the concern with morality, politics and philosophy in these plays is always subdued to the primary concern of theatricality. By allying the sublime and the grotesque, Anouilh skillfully avoids the solemnity and the boredom usually associated with the theatre of ideas. In *Le Songe du critique*, he voices his dislike for Berthold Brecht and all the so-called committed theatre, considering it, on the whole, very boring, reminding those who solemnly preach commitment of the lesson they could learn from Molière and, implicitly, from Anouilh himself: that despite everything, man can always rise above his wretched condition through laughter and defiance.[1] From *Humulus le muet* to *Le Directeur de l'Opéra*, mixing laughter and tears, Anouilh creates an entire theatrical universe based upon this essential belief.

What are the chances that this universe will survive in the years to come?

Basing his prediction on the fact that trends and fame in the history of the theatre come and go, Henri Peyre thinks that Anouilh may not go down in posterity since so few dramatists in each century do. But Peyre predicts that Anouilh will last until 1975 at least.[2]

Maurice Clavel suggests that should Anouilh survive, it will not be the moralizer of *Antigone* but the entertainer of *Le Bal des voleurs*.[3]

Gonzague Truc, on the contrary, considers that it is precisely an account of his moralizing that Anouilh has the best chances of surviving. "He will be remembered as a man who, for the pleasure of the historians to come, left a picture charged with life of days that were not beautiful, and who also recorded the futile debates of souls involved in their everyday dramas, which will delight the philosopher."[4]

When discussing the future of Molière's theatre in *Le Songe du critique,* Anouilh himself implicitly raises the question of the future of his own theatre in the midst of an increasingly scientifically oriented world, in the age of triumphant technology, in the age of the split atom and space flights. His Critic ponders, "And if tomorrow man sets foot on the moon, what will remain of Molière's theatre?"[5]

The answer to this question possibly lies within the context of Anouilh's plays in the passage in *L'Hurluberlu* in which the General expresses his belief that there are no such technical innovations as can change what is in the heart.

> Man has never changed and he never will . . . He may blow up the earthball or organize it the way he wants to, but the real problems will remain what they always have been. (131)

But even if real problems and the human heart are meant to remain forever the same, the theatre and its public do change. Already in 1953, in an article in *Arts,* writing about Beckett's *En Attendant Godot,* Anouilh recognized the advent of a new style in the theatre and praising the achievement of a rival glosses over his own limitations in all humility.[6] In 1956, in an article in *Le Figaro,* Anouilh advertised the theatrical genius of Eugène Ionesco and pleaded with the reluctant Parisian public to rush to see *Les Chaises,* thereby saving the play from closing after only a few nights.[7] But Anouilh's enthusiasm for the new theatre was short-lived. In 1959, Anouilh turned violently against the peddlers of pessimism.

It is time for the boring philosophers of despair, for
those who at regular intervals and somewhat naively
discover the horror of man's predicament, for those who
would like to prevent us from having fun in the theatre—to understand one thing: we are funny. And that
in the final analysis is more harrowing than all their
horrible descriptions of our nothingness.[8]

In *L'Hurluberlu,* Anouilh has his reactionary general deliver a harangue against all the so-called "theatre of tomorrow": "Why, it's pure hogwash . . ." (91), shouts Ludovic
who prefers Marivaux to Popopief—an inoffensive and amusing pun aimed at Ionesco, Adamov and other "new dramatists" of exotic foreign extractions.

By the end of the fifties Anouilh was well aware that
Beckett and Ionesco were capable of crystallizing and con-
veying the poetry of the stage more effectively than Giraudoux twenty or thirty years earlier. Like Giraudoux's theatre,
the theatre of Anouilh is predominantly auditive and cere-
bral, its poetry generated almost exclusively through language, which in turn serves certain attitudes and myths dear
to his heart. In comparison with the stage of Beckett in *En
Attendant Godot* and Ionesco in *Les Chaises,* Anouilh's stage
falls short when it comes to language incorporated in objects
and gestures. But it would be out of place to hold against
Anouilh the fact that he belongs to one literary tradition and
not to another one, to reproach him for not writing the kind
of plays that with all that made up his childhood, youth and
mature years he could never have written. He was enough of
a gentleman of the theatre to help promote what he thought
to be best in the new theatre. Later, when much that was
blatantly mediocre came to invade the stage hiding under the

for a while fashionable label "drama of the absurd," Anouilh began to voice his doubts about the validity of much that was being praised as the ultimate in theatre. Finally he shrugged away the existence of the avant-garde with the simple remark that nothing ages so fast as the new. Still, the avant-garde compelled Anouilh to assert with added conviction his role of provider of entertainment—light as in *Le Bal des voleurs* or more serious as when in plays like *Antigone* and *L'Alouette* he ventures into boulevard metaphysics. Often Anouilh exaggerates when claiming to be no more than a skillful manufacturer of solid theatrical merchandise geared to appeal to the market, but it is true that within these limits he can withstand any criticism whatsoever from whatever side it may come.

For thirty years, year after year, Anouilh has been peopling the stage with one René after another, each in his own way craving for or lamenting the loss of his Amélie and each reprimanded for his excessive romantic ambitions by an argumentative Father Souel. For thirty years, through bedroom as well as metaphysical farces, Anouilh has been providing us with his orchestration of the eternal debate between the body and the soul. The question of whether the philosopher is going to outlive the entertainer or the entertainer the philosopher does not seem very relevant in determining Anouilh's place in the history of modern theatre. One may at the very best express the wish that it be the philosopher, the historian and the moralizer of *Antigone* and *Pauvre Bitos,* the author so close to Camus, so fond of rebellion in the face of man's and nature's indifference to man. One may hope that the one who will endure the longer will be the chronicler, the journalist and the witness of hard times during and after World War Two, whose voice rises in indignation before certain historical crimes and yet always remains stylized, elegant and perfectly allied to the action on stage.

Contrary to the "new dramatists" who cultivate distantiation from their works, Anouilh is the type of playwright who pours all his life into his plays, crying, laughing, vituperating, battling, confessing, telling in transposition the story of his childhood, youth, old age, his loves, his disappointments, expressing thoughts about his own theatre. It may very well be, as Anouilh's Playwrights admit, that such theatre often exhibits cheap sentimentality, is talkative, abounds in locker-room jokes, relies on vaudeville gimmicks—yet in so doing it is only true to life. Anouilh works in the twilight zone between light and darkness, laughter and tears, coarse humor and elevated thoughts, part Feydeau, part Pascal.[9] He belongs to a very old tradition, the one that gave Shakespeare and Molière.[10] The theatrical historian will be likely to say that the thirties in which Anouilh began his career as playwright were most prominently marked by Giraudoux and Cocteau, the forties by Sartre and Camus, the fifties by Ionesco, Beckett and Genet. Yet Anouilh is the only outstanding French playwright who in his own sphere exercised a steady influence during all three of these decades. The true reason for his withdrawal during most of the sixties, the decade of "new criticism" rather than "new theatre," remains open to conjecture. It seems unlikely that for six years he would have offered no new play because of an alleged disagreement with De Gaulle. At the time of *La Foire d'Empoigne* Anouilh was fifty-one, the age when Molière died, the age also when "one no longer has the right to speak to young girls."[11] Was it simply a crisis of aging? A respectful silence in honor of Molière? Did he take time off to pay a debt to Shakespeare by translating and adapting four of his plays?[12] Did he feel that after thirty years of full-time work as a "manufacturer of plays" he deserved "some more time for bicycle riding" like his Playwright in *Les Poissons rouges?* Or did he wisely write for the drawer waiting for the "theatre of the absurd" to reach an impasse, so that his silence would be more noticeable and his return more festive? By 1968, when Anouilh's name reappeared on the roster of first performances, the "theatre of tomorrow" of the fifties was already largely a matter of the past. Beckett with his slender theatrical opus had become a classic like Racine. Genet also seemed to have given all he would give to the theatre. Arrabal's *L'Architecte et l'Empereur d'Assyrie,* one of the most interesting plays of the sixties, performed in Paris in 1967, sounded like a distant echo and an imitation of the fifties. There was some ferment in the late sixties. Among other attempts, particularly after the May 1968 disorders in Paris, certain directors schooled on Artaud and Brecht sought to revamp the idea of a theatre for the masses. But Ionesco was right in proclaiming that outside of some elementary experimentation with theatrical techniques which yielded some interesting results, the sixties had nothing essentially new to offer.[13] 1968 seemed the perfect moment for Anouilh to return and in doing so to exemplify that in the case of genius the barriers between old and new, tradition and adventure are almost inexistant.

Early in 1972, in the midst of much mediocre theatre, two outstanding plays were performed—Ionesco's *Macbett* and Anouilh's modern version of the Orestes story *Tu étais si gentil quand tu étais petit.* It is probably the play whose completion and performance filled Anouilh with the greatest satisfaction since for over twenty years he had been unable to go beyond a fragment of *Oreste* published in 1945. Anouilh,

embarking on his fifth decade of playwriting, thereby added
still another masterpiece to those of his plays that contain a
commentary on our times and man's fate in general. Ionesco
and Anouilh, much closer to one another than it seemed in
the fifties and sixties, appear in the early seventies as two
unsurpassable   masters   of   the   metaphysical   boulevard.
Anouilh's *Becket* and Ionesco's *La Soif et la faim* have
entered the repertory of the Comédie-Française. In the light
of these facts, if today one were to play prophet it would
seem justified to say that for many years the chances of
reviving Anouilh, Beckett and Ionesco are likely to be equal.
For traditions that remain young and avant-gardes that age
fast both live together for a long time as classic repertory.

## 9. AN ALPHABET OF ANOUILH

AGE

What would you like for your birthday?—One year less. (CHER ANTOINE)

God turns away from men over forty. (ORNIFLE)

With a foot in the grave men realize how incredibly careless they have been—how they have let happiness slip by. (LES POISSONS ROUGES)

Angels age fast and one morning you wake up and find on the pillow next to you an old angel's head in curlers. (ARDÈLE)

Faces mean nothing. It is the souls that have wrinkles. (CHER ANTOINE)

CHILDREN

Children are specialists in child's talk. The little foxes! (NE RÉVEILLEZ PAS MADAME)

CONVERSATIONS

People believe they are responding to one another while carrying on monologues instead. Everywhere we hear conversations between deaf people. (NE RÉVEILLEZ PAS MADAME)

CYNICS

The cynics are the quickest to be moved to tears. ( CHER ANTOINE)

DEATH

We are in the same train compartment and there is someone who exits at each station. So let's share our last sandwiches and talk about the scenery in order to forget the terminus. (CHER ANTOINE)

DIVORCE

Why divorce? To change reproaches? I believe in the indissolubility of marriage: it's the only guarantee one has not to be a fool twice. (LES POISSONS ROUGES)

FEELINGS

I am too worn out to be afraid of my feelings. (AR-DÈLE)

Everything changes in life. Why do you want feelings alone not to change? (NE RÉVEILLEZ PAS MADAME)

FRANCE

I can't be choosy. I am the stomach of France. I have to digest everything. (LA FOIRE D'EMPOIGNE)

The anonymous letter is our epic song. (LES POISSONS ROUGES)

During the Occupation one half of the French people denounced the other half. After the Liberation the other half denounced the first half. Some reliable historians wonder whether it was not the same half that denounced in both instances. (LES POISSONS ROUGES)

FRIENDSHIP

Friendship is a curious animal—one that bites when dead. (BECKET)

We were twenty. At that age one still believes in friends. (NE RÉVEILLEZ PAS MADAME)

## G E N I U S
It is always a pity not to possess genius. Ultimately however it is not as important as one may think. It suffices that others believe you are in possession of it. (ORNIFLE)

## G E N T L E M A N
A gentleman must always let himself be cheated a little. Up to the point of his honor, not further. (LES POISSONS ROUGES)

## G O D
God is not with the strongest but with the bravest. He doesn't like those who are afraid. (L'ALOUETTE)

## G O O D  I N T E N T I O N S
Everyone has good intentions but there is not much to be done with them. (CHER ANTOINE)

## H O U S E W I V E S
Housewives are the living image of death. Day after day, year after year untiringly they clean the same little corner overpowered every evening by newly formed dust. They wear themselves out at the task, dry up, acquire wrinkles, deteriorate, bend until that evening when, totally drained after a last cleaning, they die. Next day in the same little corner a new layer of dust shows itself. (ROMÉO ET JEANNETTE)

## H U S B A N D S
A husband is a husband. Despite all the disagreements,

even if you no longer talk to one another, he's still yours.
(LES POISSONS ROUGES)

## I D E A L S

Those who tell you that youth needs ideals are fools.
They have one: the phenomenal diversity of life, their private
life, the only true life. It is old men who need stimulation:
they thrive on ideas and young people die for them. (LA
FOIRE D'EMPOIGNE)

## I M B E C I L E S

One is never cruel enough with imbeciles. (ORNIFLE)

## I N D I V I D U A L S

Having the right to vote and owning a television set
doesn't make a man an individual. (LES POISSONS
ROUGES)

## I N T E L L E C T U A L S

All the flow of the intellectuals' saliva never modified a
single fact. (LES POISSONS ROUGES)

## L I F E

Life is never worth the trouble one takes in living it.
(ORNIFLE)

If that's life they should have told me in advance: I
would not have bothered to come. (LE BOULANGER, LA
BOULANGÈRE ET LE PETIT MITRON)

Life is a long family dinner—tedious, like all family din-
ners, but necessary. (LA VALSE DES TORÉADORS)

I was humiliated, scoffed at, cheated. I lived. (LA FOIRE
D'EMPOIGNE)

Life is definitely unreal. First of all it lacks form: no one knows his text and everyone misses his entrance. One should never leave the theatre! That is the only place where life makes some sense. (CHER ANTOINE)

We are too hard to please. Life is made up of pennies and dimes and there is a treasureful for those who know how to pick them up. But these are too small for us. We wait for life to pay us back in hundreds and thousands. So we stand poor before the treasure-vaults. (ARDÈLE)

## LITERATURE

Noble literature is even more disgusting than the other kind. It corrupts everything by giving men ideas. (NE RÉVEILLEZ PAS MADAME)

## LOVE

Had God wanted love to be lasting, I am sure he would have made desire last too. (ARDÈLE)

Love spoiled you one evening—now it's time to pay the bill. They are generous—they give you plenty of time to settle the account. Sometimes an entire life. (ARDÈLE)

## MAN

Don't think that after the stab of *Tartuffe* the hypocrites felt less at ease. Man is a solid monster. (CHER ANTOINE)

## MARRIAGE

I did not commit suicide. I got married. (CHER ANTOINE)

It is always absurd to get married. (LES POISSONS ROUGES)

Marriage is a delightful thing! One should get married all the time. (LES POISSONS ROUGES)

## MASTERPIECES

It takes professors to believe that masterpieces are the result of hard work and application. Masterpieces in the theatre are made like everything else, in a hurry, to amuse people, with God lending a helping hand in the process. Shakespeare in his day had no idea that he was writing Hamlet! He was piecing together a play for his company, a play to be rehearsed fifteen days later, that's all. (NE RÉ-VEILLEZ PAS MADAME)

## MIRRORS

One must ignore mirrors. They are traps for the weak. For my part I contemplate myself only in my old portraits painted by the best artists of the time. (CHER ANTOINE)

## NOVELISTS

Novelists have it easy: they are free to speak in place of their characters. (LA GROTTE)

## OTHERS

If one had to admire all the people one associates with, it would be impossible to have parties. (PAUVRE BITOS)

## PARIS

How beautiful Paris is, empty. It is the Parisians who spoil it. (LE BOULANGER, LA BOULANGÈRE ET LE PETIT MITRON)

PARTY

Instead of becoming a priest I joined the party. (LES POISSONS ROUGES)

PHILANTHROPISTS

The faces of true egoists are bearable; we know the game, we are all here to play it—but the faces of the philanthropists are repugnant. One does not have the right to be egoistical to such a degree! (ORNIFLE)

PLEASURE

You too will love pleasure and you'll make others suffer. Or else they'll devour you alive. (LES POISSONS ROUGES)

POLITICS

I never discuss politics or love. For centuries nothing was said about these matters. Only since people have begun discussing them has everything gone wrong. Before, politics were the concern of politicians, love the concern of whores. And believe me, they knew their business. Today everyone wants to be a politican and everyone wants to be a whore. (LES POISSONS ROUGES)

POOR PEOPLE

The poor are the most egoistical people! They have persuaded themselves once and for all that they have nothing to give; but that in turn everyone owes them something. (LES POISSONS ROUGES)

PRETENSE

To live means to pretend. It is not only actors who

pretend! Judges pretend, priests pretend, generals pretend. And they are often less gifted than actors. (NE RÉVEILLEZ PAS MADAME)

There is a game to be played according to certain rules and everyone must participate in it or else everything falls to pieces. (LA GROTTE)

R E A L I T Y

Reality is almost always base. (PAUVRE BITOS)

R E B E L L I O N

One must do against all odds what one has been given to do—to the very end. (BECKET)

R I C H   P E O P L E

Little boys from rich families are usually abandoned and they pay very dearly for the privilege of having had governesses. (LES POISSONS ROUGES)

S O C I A L   S E C U R I T Y

Can't man be trusted to his own devices? He is fed up with social security! He no longer dares to emit a fart unless sure to be reimbursed. (LES POISSONS ROUGES)

S O L I T U D E

It is abominable to be alone. One is in bad company. (CHER ANTOINE)

S T R A T E G Y

Understanding your enemy is the surest way of losing a war. (CHER ANTOINE)

STUDENTS

When you saw your father work hard all his life you wanted to have soft hands at all costs. That's why the masses more and more become students. (LES POISSONS ROUGES)

SUFFERING

Others adore to suffer. Why complicate our lives by depriving them of that pleasure. (ORNIFLE)

THEATRE

Away from the stage there is no salvation! (CHER ANTOINE)

In the theatre only the whores know how to play the saint. (NE RÉVEILLEZ PAS MADAME)

It is generally in the plays that one was unable to write that one had the most to say. (LA GROTTE)

Theatre is no more than a situation, characters plus conversation! After an hour or so there is an intermission and candies are sold in the lobby. All the rest is literature. (CHER ANTOINE)

TRAITORS

The only kind of men you can buy are those who are for sale—those who need not be feared anyway. (BECKET)

TRUTH

One must never tell the truth: it's the source of all trouble. (LES POISSONS ROUGES)

Truth is a dossier that holds together. (LA GROTTE)

WOMEN

One must content oneself with each woman's little specialty without ever asking for more. (NE RÉVEILLEZ PAS MADAME)

Women don't appreciate the theatre at all. Once they are not performing themselves, they no longer enjoy it. (LA RÉPÉTITION)

I know that women, who rather easily abandon all sorts of things hardly ever abandon a role. (NE RÉVEILLEZ PAS MADAME)

The more honest women are, the more reproachful they become later. (NE RÉVEILLEZ PAS MADAME)

Under stress, in exile, during epidemics, men falter like flies. Women, they endure. They are all fragile, cute, ailing, but don't misjudge them, they are adaptable. They make solid widows. (NE RÉVEILLEZ PAS MADAME)

YOUTH

At twenty everyone has a future. (LE BOULANGER, LA BOULANGÈRE ET LE PETIT MITRON)

## NOTES AND REFERENCES

### 1. Gradus ad Parnassum

1 Charles Dullin remained the most active member of the "Cartel" during the Occupation years. He moved out of the Atelier to become co-director of the Théâtre de Paris and shortly afterwards director of the Théâtre Sarah Bernhardt, where he had the courage to present Sartre's *Les Mouches* in 1943. After the death of Pitoëff in 1939, the "Cartel," which had held a preponderant sway over the theatrical life in Paris in the thirties, lost ground and continued to do so during the Occupation. Jouvet, urged by the authorities to leave France, agreed to make a South American tour, from which he returned only after his country's Liberation. Gaston Baty was less active. During the 1942-43 season, he even turned over the direction of his Théâtre Montparnasse to the great interpreter of Racine, Marguerite Jamois.

2 Gabriel Marcel, "Sartre, Anouilh et le problème de Dieu," *La Nouvelle Revue canadienne*, I, 4 (September-October 1951), 35-36.

3 Under the directorship of Marguerite Jamois the following plays by Anouilh have been performed at the Théâtre Montparnasse-Gaston Baty: *L'Alouette* (1953), *Pauvre Bitos ou Le Dîner de têtes* (1956), *Becket ou L'Honneur de Dieu* (1959), and *La Grotte* (1961).

4 Hubert Gignoux, *Jean Anouilh*, p. 9.

5 André Parinaud, "Talk with Anouilh," *New York Times*, CVI, 36, 149 (January 13, 1957), Section Two, pp. 1, 3.

6 Roland Laudenbach, "Anouilh cinéaste," *Cahiers de la Compagnie Madeleine Renaud—Jean-Louis Barrault*, No. 26 (May 1959), p. 44.

7  Marcel Aymé, "Jean Anouilh le mystérieux," *Livres de France*, No. 8 (October 1960), p. 4.

8  Robert de Luppé, *Jean Anouilh*, p. 11.

## 2. Rebellion against Time

1  *Pièces roses: Humulus le muet* (1929), *Le Bal des voleurs* (1932), *Le Rendez-vous de Senlis* (1937), *Léocadia* (1939).

*Pièces brillantes: L'Invitation au château* (1947), *Colombe* (1950), *Le Répétition ou L'Amour puni* (1950), *Cécile ou L'Ecole des pères* (1949).

Two of the *Pièces grinçantes: Ardèle ou La Marguerite* (1948), *La Valse des toréadors* (1951).

2  The only two settings that strike discordant notes among the otherwise harmonious and highly stylized decors of the *Pièces roses, Pièces brillantes* and two of the *Pièces grinçantes* are a linen room in the second act of *Le Rendez-vous de Senlis* and a small attic room in the fourth act of *La Répétition.* At the Paris performance of *La Répétition,* the attic room scene was transposed into the same elegant drawing room where the rest of the play takes place. In a note on p. 422 of *La Répétition,* Anouilh admits that the play gains in unity from this change, although it was not originally foreseen by him.

3  In *Le Bal des voleurs,* three thieves are invited to the villa of Lady Hurf. One of the invited thieves, Gustave, falls in love with Lady Hurf's niece Juliette. Gustave is thus the only male *invité au chateau* in the *Pièces roses* and *Pièces brillantes.*

4  The life model for Léocadia's "death by the scarf" was the extravagant death in 1927 of the American actress Isadora Duncan, vividly described by Dos Passos in *The Big Money,* the third volume of *U.S.A.*:

she got in beside him and

she threw her heavilyfringed scarf round her neck with a big sweep she had and

turned back and said,
with the strong California accent her French never lost:
Adieu, mes amis, je vais à la gloire.
The mechanic put his car in gear and started.
The heavy trailing scarf caught in a wheel, wound tight. Her head was wrenched against the side of the car. The car stopped instantly; her neck was broken, her nose crushed, Isadora was dead.

5 The Prince has purchased and brought into his garden the following living and silent witnesses of the three unforgettable days spent with Léocadia: a taxi with its driver, who gave them a ride; an ice cream vendor who sold them ice cream; an entire orchestra, witnesses to their dancing; and even a municipal park bench on which they rested for a while. Every morning, the Prince strolls disconsolately through his graveyard of memories.

6 Leonard Cabell Pronko, *The World of Jean Anouilh* (Berkeley and Los Angeles, 1961), p. 93.

### 3. Rebellion against Environment

1 From now on whenever we say *Pièces noires* we shall have in mind both the *Pièces noires* and the *Nouvelles Pièces noires*, with the exception of *Antigone* and *Médée*, two plays that within the context of our analysis belong to a different category.

2 In the *Pièces noires*, when not exploring the universe of the poverty-stricken, Anouilh takes us into homes belonging to the upper bourgeoisie: Florent's home in Acts II and III of *La Sauvage* and the rich provincial bougeois home of the Renauds in *Le Voyageur sans bagage*. Both the cheap rooms of the poor and the elegant rooms of the upper bourgeois are far removed from the drawing rooms in the sumptuous castles surrounded by gardens in the *Pièces roses* and *Pièces brillantes*.
The only play among the *Pièces noires* in which the action is set in a castle is *L'Hermine*. In this play, however, the castle serves an entirely different purpose from that of the castles in the *Pièces roses* and *Pièces*

*brillantes.* In *L'Hermine,* the castle accentuates the contrast between the protagonist's poverty and the milieu to which the girl he loves belongs. It does not shelter a frivolous dream or an idle game as in the case of the castles in the *Pièces roses* and *Pièces brillantes.*

4  Robert Kemp, *La Vie du théâtre* (Paris, 1956), p. 89.

### 4. Rebellion for a Cause

1 One day Reverend Father Doncoeur, author of a book in which the life of Joan of Arc is retraced day by day, from the first revelation of the Voices to her burning at the stake, came to thank Anouilh for having helped him with the dialogues for a film on Joan's life.

At that occasion Father Doncoeur suggested: "And if you were to write a play about Joan?" whereupon Anouilh answered, "I have already written a play about Antigone." Father Doncoeur retorted, "Precisely, Joan is the Christian Antigone."

The conversation with Father Doncoeur which incited Anouilh to write *L'Alouette* is related in Anouilh's article "Une inexplicable joie . . . " reprinted in Pol Vandromme's *Jean Anouilh, un auteur et ses personnages,* p. 221.

2 In *The Lark,* her adaptation of *L'Alouette,* Lillian Hellman altogether eliminated Joan's father from the play's ending. She also rewrote the role of La Hire, betraying Anouilh's intentions. In *L'Alouette,* at the time when Joan still hopes that he will deliver her from her Rouen prison, La Hire, her best friend and companion in arms lingers in Germany in search of new military employment. In *The Lark* Lillian Hellman has him return just in time to embellish the happy ending with his presence and pronounce a few contrived, reassuring remarks. *The Lark,* adapted by Lillian Hellman, in *Jean Anouilh* (Five Plays), II (New York, 1959) 301-2.

3 Jean Anouilh, "Mystère de Jeanne," reprinted in Pol Vandromme's *Jean Anouilh, un auteur et ses personnages,* pp. 236-37, translated in *The Genius of the French Theatre,* edited by Albert Bermel (New York, 1961), p. 444.

4 For the historical background of *Becket,* Anouilh relied almost entirely on the thirty pages on Becket's life in Augustin Thierry's *Conquest of England by the Normans.* Having completed *Becket,* Anouilh gave the manuscript to an historian friend to read. The verdict was disappointing. The historian poked fun at Anouilh for having made Becket into a Saxon, when, for the past fifty years, ever since the time of Augustin Thierry, it has been proved and authoritatively upheld that Becket was not a Saxon but a Norman from a town in the vicinity of Rouen called Bequet.

Although an important part of Anouilh's play was based on the fact that Becket was a Saxon, Anouilh refused to do any rewriting. For the play he had written, it was much better that Becket be a Saxon. He therefore decided that if history were to make further progress in the coming fifty years it might perhaps rediscover that Becket was indeed a Saxon. Notes Anouilh: "I changed nothing; I had the play performed three months later in Paris. It had a great success and I noticed that no one except my historian friend was aware of the progress of history." For Anouilh's writing of *Becket,* see the Introduction to *Becket or The Honor of God,* translated by Lucienne Hill (New York, 1960).

## 5. Historical Rebellion

1 Jean Anouilh, *Fables,* pp. 114-15.

## 6. Rebellion without a Cause

1 A word concocted by Anouilh to designate a courage-inspiring piece of red blotter, used in several of his plays.

2 In his article, "Les Hurluberlus parallèles," *Ecrits de Paris,* March 1959, pp. 112-18, Claude Jamet compares Ludovic in *L'Hurluberlu* with Molière's Alceste in *Le Misanthrope* and Arnolphe in *L'Ecole des femmes.* Ludovic is an Alceste who has reached Arnolphe's age. He is the fifty-year-old lover who has the support of both the spectator and the author. Jamet points to the change in attitude toward old age on the part of Anouilh, close to fifty himself at the time he wrote

*L'Hurluberlu.* In plays like *La Sauvage, Antigone, L'Alouette,* youth has the monopoly on ideals, and the aged characters are repulsive or ridiculous. In *L'Hurluberlu* it is the young ones who are repulsive and ridiculous, while an old man evokes the ideal. In the course of the play, the general calls himself · "a young man on his decline." Notes Jamet with amusement and irony: "With the coming of old age, Anouilh had simply discovered that youth is not necessarily an attribute of the young."

### 7. Rebellion of the Artist

1 It is appropriate to draw a parallel between *La Répétition ou L'Amour puni* and *Cher Antoine ou L'Amour raté.* In *La Répétition* love is punished at the end of the play, in *Cher Antoine* it is an acknowledged failure from the outset. The two friends, Antoine who is fifty and Marcelin who is fifty-one, are Tigre and Héro thirteen years later.

2 Camomille, Antoine's fifteen-year-old daughter in *Les Poissons rouges* marries Gérard Courtepointe, the teen-age son of a wealthy manufacturer of plastic products.

3 The symbol of the hunchback in *Les Poissons rouges* can be compared to the symbol of the rhinoceros in Ionesco's *Rhinocéros.* They both illustrate the degradation of man in modern society.

4 Albert Camus, *The Myth of Sisyphus* (New York, 1959), p. 84.

5 Allusion to the last line of *La Grotte,* a play about a play's making in which the Playwright on stage perpetually runs after his characters who often escape his control and take him in directions he had not originally intended. At the end the Playwright turns to the spectators and says: "Ladies and gentlemen, please excuse the Playwright's blunders. But this play he was never able to write."

## 8. Conclusion

1 Jean Anouilh, *Le Songe du critique*, *L'Avant-Scène*, No. 243 (May 15, 1961).

2 Henri Peyre, *Contemporary French Literature. A Critical Anthology* (New York, 1964), p. 291.

3 "Jean Anouilh deviendra-t-il un auteur classique?" *Arts*, No. 836 (September 27-October 3, 1961), p. 5.

4 Gonzague Truc, "Jean Anouilh et le théâtre du refus," *Ecrits de Paris*, No. 45 (July 1948), p. 147.

5 *Le Songe du critique*, p. 32.

6 Jean Anouilh, "Godot ou Le Sketch des *Pensées* de Pascal traité par les Fratellini," *Arts*, No. 400 (February 27-March 5, 1953), p. 1.

7 Jean Anouilh, "Du Chapitre des *Chaises*," *Le Figaro*, April 23, 1956.

8 Jean Anouilh, "Présence de Molière," *L'Avant-Scène*, No. 210 (December 15, 1959), p. 8.

9 In *Le Boulanger, la Boulangère et le Petit Mitron*, Adolphe commenting on tragedy and comedy says: "All put together, vaudeville alone remains tragic and true to real life. Feydeau is the only one who truly depicted man's condition . . . And Pascal."

10 At the end of *Les Poissons rouges*, The Playwright Antoine reminds his son Toto in the course of a bicycle ride, that he is an heir to the noblest tradition of mankind, perpetrated through its best representatives. Among these are Shakespeare, Molière and Pascal.

11 This thought along with some other similar ones concerning the

impasse of being "fifty," is expressed by the Playwright Antoine in *Cher Antoine.*

12  In 1964 Anouilh adapted Shakespeare's *Richard III* and translated and adapted *As You Like It, A Winter's Tale* and *Twelfth Night.*

13  Ionesco expresses conclusive thoughts about the state of the French theatre in the sixties in his preface to Thomas Bishop's anthology *L'Avant-garde théâtrale* (New York, 1970).

## CHRONOLOGY OF THEATRICAL PRODUCTIONS

1932 *L'Hermine* (Théâtre de l'Oeuvre)

1933 *Mandarine* (Théâtre de l'Athénée)

1935 *Y avait un prisonnier* (Théâtre des Ambassadeurs)

1937 *Le Voyageur sans bagage* (Théâtre des Mathurins)

1938 *La Sauvage* (Théâtre des Mathurins)

1938 *Le Bal des voleurs* (Théâtre des Arts)

1940 *Léocadia* (Théâtre de la Michodière)

1941 *Le Rendez-vous de Senlis* (Théâtre de l' Atelier)

1942 *Eurydice* (Théâtre de l'Atelier)

1944 *Antigone* (Théâtre de l'Atelier)

1946 *Roméo et Jeannette* (Théâtre de l'Atelier)

1947 *L'Invitation au château* (Théâtre de l'Atelier)

1948 *Episode de la vie d'un auteur* (Comédie des Champs-Elysées)
    Presented as a curtain raiser with *Ardèle ou La Marguerite*

1948 *Ardèle ou La Marguerite* (Comédie des Champs-Elysées)

1950 *La Répétition ou L'Amour puni* (Théâtre Marigny)

1951 *Colombe* (Théâtre de l'Atelier)

1952 *La Valse des toréadors* (Comédie des Champs-Elysées)

1953 *Médée* (Théâtre de l'Atelier)

1953 *L'Alouette* (Théâtre Montparnasse-Gaston Baty)

1954 *Cécile ou L'Ecole des pères* (Comédie des Champs-Elysées)

1955 *Ornifle ou Le Courant d'air* (Comédie des Champs-Elysées)

1956 *Pauvre Bitos ou Le Dîner de têtes* (Théâtre Montparnasse-Gaston Baty)

1959 *L'Hurluberlu ou Le Réactionnaire amoureux* (Comédie des Champs-Elysées)

1959 *La Petite Molière* (Théâtre de France)

1959 *Becket ou L'Honneur de Dieu* (Théâtre Montparnasse-Gaston Baty)

1960 *Le Songe du critique* (Comédie des Champs-Elysées)
Presented as a curtain raiser with Molière's *Tartuffe* directed by Anouilh

1961 *La Grotte* (Théâtre Montparnasse-Gaston Baty)

1962 *L'Orchestre* (Comédie des Champs-Elysées)

1962 *La Foire d'Empoigne* (Comédie des Champs-Elysées)

1968 *Le Boulanger, la Boulangère et le Petit Mitron* (Comédie des Champs-Elysées)

1969 *Cher Antoine ou L'Amour raté* (Comédie des Champs-Elysées)

1970 *Les Poissons rouges ou "Mon Père ce héros"* (Théâtre de l'Oeuvre)

1970 *Ne réveillez pas Madame* (Comédie des Champs-Elysées)

1972 *Tu étais si gentil quand tu étais petit* (Théâtre Antoine)

1972 *Le Directeur de l'Opéra* (Comédie des Champs-Elysées)

## PUBLISHED PLAYS OF JEAN ANOUILH
## AS OF DECEMBER 1972

### IN COLLECTIONS

1. *Pièces roses* (*Humulus le muet, Le Bal des voleurs, Le Rendez-vous de Senlis, Léocadia*). Paris: La Table Ronde, 1958.

2. *Pièces noires* (*L'Hermine, La Sauvage, Le Voyageur sans bagage, Eurydice*). Paris: La Table Ronde, 1958.

3. *Nouvelles Pièces noires* (*Jézabel, Antigone, Roméo et Jeannette, Médée*). Paris: La Table Ronde, 1958.

4. *Pièces brillantes* (*L'Invitation au château, Colombe, La Répétition ou L'Amour puni, Cécile ou L'Ecole des pères*). Paris: La Table Ronde, 1960.

5. *Pièces grinçantes* (*Ardèle ou La Marguerite, La Valse des toréadors, Ornifle ou Le Courant d'air, Pauvre Bitos on Le Dîner de têtes*). Paris: La Table Ronde, 1958.

6. *Pièces costumées* (*L'Alouette, Becket ou L'Honneur de Dieu, La Foire d'Empoigne*). Paris: La Table Ronde, 1960.

7. *Nouvelles Pièces grinçantes* (*L'Hurluberlu ou Le Réactionnaire amoureux, La Grotte, L'Orchestre, Le Boulanger, la Boulangère et le Petit Mitron, Les Poissons rouges ou "Mon Père ce héros"*). Paris: La Table Ronde, 1970.

### STILL IN SEPARATE EDITIONS:

1. *Episode de la vie d'un auteur. Cahiers de la Compagnie Madeleine Renaud—Jean-Louis Barrault*, No. 26 (May 1959), pp. 61-96.

2. *La Petite Molière. L'Avant-Scène*, No. 210 (December 15, 1959), pp. 10-42.

3. *Le Songe du critique. L'Avant-Scène*, No. 243 (May 15, 1961), pp. 31-35.

4. *Cher Antoine ou L'Amour raté.* Paris: La Table Ronde, 1969.
5. *Ne réveillez pas Madame.* Paris: La Table Rounde, 1970.
6. *Tu étais si gentil quand tu étais petit.* Paris: La Table Ronde, 1972.
7. *Le Directeur de l'Opéra.* Paris: La Table Ronde, 1972.

## SELECTED BIBLIOGRAPHY OF
## BOOKS AND ARTICLES ON ANOUILH

BOOKS

Fazia, Alba della. *Jean Anouilh.* New York: Twayne Publishers, 1969.

Gignoux, Hubert. *Jean Anouilh.* Paris: Editions du Temps Présent, 1946.

Luppé, Robert de. *Jean Anouilh.* Paris: Editions Universitaires, 1959.

Pronko, Leonard Cabell. *The World of Jean Anouilh.* Berkeley and Los Angeles: University of California Press, 1961.

Vandromme, Pol. *Jean Anouilh, un auteur et ses personnages.* Paris: La Table Ronde, 1965.

ARTICLES:

Aymé, Marcel. "Jean Anouilh le mystérieux," *Livres de France,* No. 8 (October 1960), pp. 2-4.

Champigny, Robert. "Theatre in a Mirror: Anouilh," *Yale French Studies,* No. 14 (Winter 1954/1955), pp. 57-64.

Truc, Gonzague. "Jean Anouilh et le théâtre du refus," *Ecrits de Paris,* No. 45 (July 1948), pp. 88-92.

Truc, Gonzague. "M. Anouilh, dramaturge et moraliste," *Ecrits de Paris,* No. 163 (September 1958), pp. 144-150.